Change
or Decay

Change
or Decay

Irish Catholicism in crisis

Brendan Hoban

Also by Brendan Hoban

Personally Speaking
The Lisnagoola Chronicles
Sermons for Special Occasions
A Touch of the Heart

For Moya, Martha and Patrick

CONTENTS

Foreword: Saying the awkward word 9

1   A time for laughter, a time for tears 13

2   The triumph of failure 23

3   Change just is 33

4   Keeping reality at bay 45

5   The tyranny of clericalism 57

6   The divine conspiracy 71

7   Priesthood at the heart of darkness 81

8   The care of priests? 93

9   Celibacy: the strangled impulse 105

10 Authority in decline 115

11 New kinds of leader 123

12 The way we worship 135

13 Spirituality 147

14 Yesterday was always best 159

15 The morning after optimism 167

FOREWORD

Saying the Awkward Word

It is a sense of loyalty to the gospel and to the institutional church that often prompts the breaking of an unholy silence, that brings a man or woman to speak respectfully and directly to church authorities and others about what matters to them most. It is a sense of loyalty that prompts members of the faithful - laity, religious, priests, bishops - to call for discussion of issues that may indeed be dangerous to face but that ultimately will be more dangerous to the church if not faced.

Donald Cozzens

One of the priest's first services to the world is to tell the truth.

Cardinal Suhard

DONALD Cozzens begins his book, *Sacred Silence: Denial and the Crisis in the Church*, by asking the question: 'What are we afraid of?' It is a fair question, a question that the Irish Catholic Church needs to ask itself.

What are we afraid of? hides a hundred other questions: Why is the Irish Catholic Church so out of touch with the lived experience of its people? Why have we so much difficulty with concepts like accountability and democracy? Why was the energy and vision of the

Vatican II strangled at birth? Why did the clerical church see the developing role of the laity as a threat to its power? How did so many highly intelligent, moral and committed church-people get it so wrong over child abuse? What prevents us from recognising the changing face of authority and the changing demands of church leadership? Why are we afraid to ask the hard questions about the darkness at the heart of priesthood?

From time to time in *The Furrow*, *Intercom*, *Céide* and other publications I have tried to mull over these questions. It seemed to me that they were key issues for a declining Church. Yet the official Church seemed reluctant to face the issues involved and seemed resentful that someone like myself, inside the clerical brotherhood, should have the audacity to say the awkward word.

Saying the awkward word meant exclusion from the clerical club: the resentment of my colleagues; the unwanted attention of bishops, my own and others who sought to pressure them; the confusion of my parishioners; sometimes even the hurt of family and friends.

It was a lonely place to be, outside the camp. Especially when what seemed important and obvious to say was dismissed as disloyal and unacceptable. Like an article in *The Furrow* that named a few truths about the decline of Confession and our failure to accept that unless we reconstituted the Sacrament of Reconciliation in a format that was credible to our people, we would end up with just six sacraments. A letter from the nunciature in Dublin demanded an explanation for what, to me, couldn't be more clear. Even though the article had elicited congratulatory letters from bishops (among others) praising me for my courage, I was compelled, after more than twenty-five years of priesthood, to re-state my fidelity to church and gospel. The fact that I was still around wasn't, it seemed, sufficient evidence of my orthodoxy. In the strangled procedures of officialdom I was, apparently, regarded as threat rather than gift!

The extraordinary thing about such official interventions was that while privately people in powerful positions in the Church - priests, bishops, even a future cardinal - commended me for my courage and clarity, their support didn't extend to agreeing publicly with what I had written. The lack of moral courage among bishops, in assuming their authority and credibility as pastors of their Irish flocks, vis-a-vis official reprimands from Rome is, to me, one of the wonders of the world. Who are they afraid of? What do they think the Pope will do to them? I am reminded of the famous comment of the late Bishop of Killaloe, Michael Harty who, shortly before his death, remarked that bishops had forgotten that it was possible to say No to Rome.

Or priests, who privately say one thing, but very publicly say another. If Rich, in *A Man for All Seasons,* betrayed Thomas More so that he could get his grubby hands on the principality of Wales, what price are we paying for some possible ecclesiastical Ballydehob? What have we got to lose?

Thirty years ago, when I was ordained a priest, it seemed to me that it was in the interests of the gospel and of the church to face the challenge behind the questions our Church needed to face. At that time more than ninety per cent of Catholics attended weekly Mass, seminaries were full, priests had the wind on their backs, bishops were - in some instances - the darlings of the media.

Thirty years on, a tide has gone out. The Catholic Church in Ireland is, in a number of key areas, in free-fall. Yet extraordinarily we still seem reluctant to face the truths that everyone else can now recognise. A feudal church is incapable of conversing with today's world. And unless we embrace change the Irish Catholic Church will turn over and die, unless we are prepared to move from denial to reality, from self-interest to gospel courage, from a necessary dying to a new way of living.

In these pages I want to have my say on what, I believe, that means for us now: a Church where diversity is cherished and difference celebrated rather than where tradition is static and the past is glorified; a Church which welcomes and celebrates change; a Church in tune with the rhythms of our time: a Church that honours the teachings embedded in the documents of the Second Vatican Council and implements them in the spirit intended; a Church that is prepared to name the truth, regardless; a Church that recognises the darkness within priesthood and is prepared to explore and change the church rule that links priesthood to celibacy; a Church that believes that all authority and decision-making doesn't have to be reserved for a clerical club; a Church that accepts the need for new forms of authority and leadership; a Church where respect for women goes beyond mere words; a Church where all the baptised, including the clerical Church, will find their voices and honour the melody that comes from the symphony of voices that God intended his Church to be.

Brendan Hoban,
Kilglass,
Enniscrone,
Co. Sligo.

Note: The phrase 'The Church' used throughout the text should more accurately be 'the Irish Roman Catholic Church' but for ease of usage the first form is used throughout.

I dedicate this book to three recent additions to my family circle of love and care, Moya Keane and Martha Hoban, my grandnieces, and Patrick Hoban, my grandnephew. Someday, I hope they will read these words and will want to be part of a rich tradition of faith, hope and love that is their heritage and their right.

CHAPTER ONE

A time for laughter, a time for tears

I shall know why - when Time is over -
And I have ceased to wonder why -
Christ will explain each separate anguish
In the fair schoolroom in the sky -
He will tell me what 'Peter' promised -
And I - for wonder at his woe -
I shall forget the drop of Anguish
That scalds me now - that scalds me now!

Emily Dickinson

THERE were no comets seen that September time in 1966 when eighty-four young men arrived in St Patrick's College, Maynooth to begin our study for the priesthood. It was, we were told, a smaller than usual complement - the previous year the figure had exceeded one hundred. I was eighteen years of age at the time and full of the bright certainty of youth. Paddy Walkin, I remember, had pulled his Volkswagen van to the side of the front gates, as if reluctant to enter holy ground, and deposited five first-years from Killala diocese and our assorted belongings.

A week earlier we had been interviewed by Bishop Patrick O'Boyle. At one stage during the proceedings he had asked us to kneel before him and repeat some Latin formulas. Later we learned that, suffering from some form of senility, he had been under the impression that we were newly-ordained priests and, as the custom then was, had insisted that we swear an oath against 'Modernism', a putative heresy that suggested that Catholicism was not incompatible with modernity. (Later a friend wryly remarked that since I didn't know what I was doing, I felt dispensed for life from its requirements.)

So on that bright September day I found myself walking through the side gate of Maynooth College under the huge oak trees in a black suit, a Mr. Sandeman black overcoat, a black hat and carrying a huge case in which a long black soutane was carefully folded. A monitor, a final year student, was there to greet us. He handed me a little black book with Latin prayers and asked me to sign my name on a black ledger.

A tour of the seminary followed. Silken Thomas's tree. Stoyte House. The college library. The college chapel. The swimming pool. Rhetoric House. And Number 17 Humanity House, where I was to spend my first year. Formal dress, a black soutane, was prescribed for evening tea. In a passing mirror I spied an esoteric creature swathed in black and suddenly realised it was myself. The first of an infinity of incongruities.

The next morning, the Reverend Doctor Patrick Muldoon, the on-duty dean of discipline, greeted us. 'Coldly' wouldn't do the reception justice. We were in Callan Hall and we had watched him, in soutane and toga, walk in silence to the dais, peering directly in front of him as if examining a spot on the far wall. A form of 'custody of the eyes', we concluded later on when we had got used to such novelties.

Muldoon had a kind of shuffling gait as if on castors and the fact that we couldn't see his shoes added to the fantasy that, like most of the rest of the seminary staff, he had descended through a different genetic avenue. He surveyed our group with a studied disdain. His first words were, 'Good morning, gentlemen'. *Gentlemen* - that essential Maynooth appellation that presents as respect but was a hybrid of distance, disdain and separateness. 'Gentlemen.' He repeated the word as if to get us used to its texture and meaning, 'Gentlemen, my job is to get rid of half of you'. Was this an attempt at humour, an effort to lighten the proceedings with something approaching human warmth? We weren't sure. Later we learned that levity wasn't part of his make-up. He had examined our signatures, he told us, in the ledger in the gate-lodge and had noticed that a number of students had signed themselves as Tom, Dick or Harry. A flicker of laughter from the eighty-four fresh-faced eighteen-year-olds spread across the hall but was quickly impaled on his morose, solitary stare. 'From now on gentlemen,' he said, 'nobody is Tom, Dick or Harry but Thomas, Richard or Henry'. We shivered in our black shoes. A welcome, Maynooth style. Our 'formation' had begun.

Then Muldoon distributed the traditional complement of books: Thomas a Kempis's *The Imitation of Christ*, Phillip's *Meditations*, Frances de Sales's *An Introduction to the Devout Life*, *The Liber Usualis* and a Bible. And then the Dean, whom we noticed always seemed to hang his smile on the back of the door when he came into a room, proceeded to teach us how to make the sign of peace. John McArevay, now Bishop of Dromore, was the victim. After much bobbing and weaving ('We'll try that again, Mr McArevay') he got the gist of it. Then an instruction in, mystery of mysteries, how to wear and handle a biretta, which like Gaul (in Seamus Heaney's phrase) was divided into three parts.

Seven years later on a June day, I left in bright

certainty. And in bell-bottomed denims, all the rage at the time. The black overcoat had disappeared, the soutane had turned green and was cast aside some years earlier, the hat was left on top of the wardrobe in my room in St Mary's, a wan symbol of an era that had slipped into the mists of time. And even though Muldoon was right and half the eighty-four of the '66 class had slipped away over the seven years, as I left to prepare for ordination in my own place I felt not just the same mixture of hope and excitement that generations of young priests experienced before me in that benign hiatus between seminary and ordination but a sense that I was part of a new and radically different Church.

1966 and 1973 were two different worlds, two different churches. We had arrived on the cusp of a tangible excitement with the promise of the Second Vatican Council. We sensed the change in the efforts to humanise Maynooth as a seminary, to put flesh on the insights of the conciliar documents, to give the new theology space to stand its ground and to appoint bishops like Eamonn Casey in succession to bishops like Michael Browne of Galway.

We had been told - and we had bought the promise - that the church was going to renew itself in a way that connected with the compulsions of people's lives. We had been told - and we had bought the hope - that words like *collegiality* and *co-responsibility* would be given substance, that institutions would emerge that would put flesh on the people's church of the Second Vatican Council. And we had been told - and we had bought the welcome - that we were badly needed, young and energetic shoulders to the plough.

In 1973 I was ordained into an optimistic church. The climate was fair and we had the wind on our backs. In the words of priest-poet Pádraig J. Daly:

sunlight blessed us,
fields of birds sang for us,
even the rain was 'God's kindness tangible.'

It was a time of unimaginable delight and promise. The humour and camaraderie of the seminary days had kept at bay the more outrageous narrowness that simmered under the surface of our seminary years, as staid traditions of what passed for formation tried to come to terms with the demands of a changing world. And now suddenly ordination with its attendant celebratory and supportive feel was a field of dreams opening out ahead of us. Even though we knew that silver linings often had clouds attached to them, even though we recognised the hothouse ambience of the seminary bore little comparison to the cooler surrounds of everyday parish life, we still believed that everything was possible.

It was a moment of youthful wonder, a still point in life, poised somewhere between an acute awareness of the presence of God and the certainty that a new church opened up for us. New generations were to be won for Christ and we had the energy and the zeal to do it. A new church was to be born and we had the enthusiasm and the talent to drive it. With the Bible in one hand and the documents of Vatican Two in the other. And the latest ESRI report in front of us on the desk. Or so the legend has it.

Like every period in every life, it was the best of times and the worst of times, that mixture of image and reality, truth and hypocrisy, brightness and darkness that makes up the messiness of a lived life.

Thirty years on, the perspective is different. Now we have the wind in our faces and the hill rising against us. Now teenagers are telling us that religion isn't relevant any more, and adults that becoming a priest doesn't make sense anymore. Now we are often presented in the popular media as Fr Teds or Fr Jacks or more recognisably Fr Dougals, the limited lexicon of modern clerical types, living in a carefully constructed world of our own making and oblivious to the fact that we are, more often than not, the only ones listening to our own voices. Or Brendan Smyths, inhabiting a more malign world.

We have lived through a recurring nightmare of betrayals of public and private trusts, of episcopal mal-administration, of incompetent leadership at every level, of declining congregations, of decreasing, almost disappearing vocations and of diminishing respect.

We have watched in anger and in horror as a world and a culture changed before our eyes through the stories of Eamon Casey, Michael Cleary, Brendan Smyth, Ivan Payne and others and through television programmes like *Cardinal Sins* and *Suing the Pope*.

Now even Maynooth as a seminary is a pale shadow of its former self with a total of just fifty-five students - some five hundred less than a hundred years ago - even though seminaries in Wexford, Carlow, Thurles and Kilkenny as well as Clonliffe in Dublin have closed their doors forever. And as the well continues to run dry the unthinkable is actually happening: after two-hundred years we are facing the prospect of managing Maynooth's inevitable closure as a seminary. Who would have thought it would all come to this? And now thirty years later the remnants of the class of '73 are, like Beau Geste, holding our tattered flags in the desert. What has gone wrong?

Perhaps the most obvious truth is that we have failed as a church to manage change. An apt image is that of a skier trying to hold his feet in the middle of an avalanche as the ground crumbles beneath him. Like most institutions we underestimated the intensity and the depth of change and we failed to trust those prophets who would have helped us to deal with it. We also failed to trust the vision of Vatican Two, the road-map that God left us to find our way in a changing world and that was torn up into little pieces by clerical gods who refused to accept its import. Now as the Church implodes around us we recognise the price we have paid for the philosophy and the actions of those who insisted on turning us again in the dismal direction of the model of Trent.

Thirty years after the Second Vatican Council, if we had trusted the Spirit and persevered with the dream, we would have in place a structure that would have turned our church into a lay-driven institution with a participative and collaborative ethos, a structure that would have built into it processes for dealing with the failures of the past, an analysis of the needs of the present and a method of devising strategies for the future. That didn't happen because there was a failure in leadership among the bishops and clergy, a lack of commitment to, and a palpable discomfort with, the new theology of Church and a disheartening return to an ethos of control and infallibility.

The story of the last thirty years of the Irish Church is of an inglorious betrayal of the spirit and energy that Vatican II unleashed in our church. No more and no less. We are now paying the price of centralised control by a clerical church in the decline in church authority, the distrust of wide sections of our people and the free fall in religious practice. The sheer incompetence of the clerical church in dealing with child abuse and other scandals is a telling reminder of the loss our Church has sustained by that failure in trust and imagination to resource a people's Church.

The failure, of course, is not all of our own making. It is part of the price we're paying for the restoration policy in the church universal in recent years and for a lack of courage in opposing it. For even more disconcertingly, in the wider church a great tide has turned. The effort to connect with the modern world that Vatican II represented has been sidetracked by a thousand qualifications. The new conservative 'wisdom' is that John XXIII was a bumbling old man and Paul VI a tortured soul who led the church down a cul-de-sac and

Pope John Paul II strove mightily to undo the damage
they have caused. As Peter Hebblethwaite, biographer of
John XXIII and Paul VI, has written: 'John Paul's actions
say clearly that he considers Paul VI to have been weak,
vacillating and mistaken on priestly identity, religious
life, dangerous theologians, episcopal collegiality,
ecumenism, the Ostpolitik and Vatican II'.

All around us is evidence that the legacy of John
XXIII and of Paul VI is being dismantled bit by bit. Now,
at a time when intellectual rigour and the ability to
converse with a variety of ideologies were never more
needed, theologians with open minds are no longer
appointed to positions of influence in university or
seminary. Now, for example, theologians are told they
cannot write about the ordination of women just as the
Holy Office once told Karl Rahner that he was forbidden
to write about concelebration. (When he reminded Paul
VI of this years later the Pope smiled and said 'Yes, there
is a time for laughter and a time for tears'.) Now priests
who try to put ordinary words on complex issues and
who try to translate the compassion of Christ into the
brokenness of ordinary life seem to automatically
exclude themselves from positions of leadership in our
church. Events like the Extraordinary Synod of 1985,
which abandoned the key Vatican II concept of our
understanding of the Church as 'the people of God' are
further evidence of what Peter Hebblethwaite once called
'the pessimistic re-editing of the signs of the times'.

> *Footfalls echo in memory*
> *Down the passage which we did not take*
> *Towards the door we never opened*
> *Into the rose-garden.*
> (T. S. Eliot, *The Four Quartets*)

Now we are getting back to the black and white
responses of the past. Once again we are expected to

believe that every question has an answer, every problem a solution. We are casting aside the tortured subtleties of the post-Vatican II years and retrieving a new black and white catechism world. Once more a coach and four can be driven between body and soul, Church and world.

In this book, I want to proclaim my own truth in my own words about the Church I love. John XXIII once memorably described the Church as, 'not a museum to be guarded but a garden to be cultivated'. And that makes sense to me. I don't want to live as a keeper of a museum where the past is glorified, where tradition is defined outside any contact with a living and changing world. I want to live in a garden where every variety of shade and colour has its place, where diversity is cherished and difference celebrated, where every sight and smell and nuance matter. 'We are not on earth as museum-keepers' Pope John wrote, 'but to cultivate a glorious future.'

In a strange way, in these limiting times, what I have to say in these pages may at last find someone listening. The church is imploding, the museum is falling down and those who trusted in its power, resilience and certainties may now out of necessity, even desperation, be more inclined to consider the inconvenience and unreason of a garden. Where else can we go now that we have learned to our horror the price we have paid in not taking God at His word?

CHAPTER TWO
The triumph of failure

All too often the new wine of Vatican II was put into old wineskins and as we know those old wine skins have been bursting all around us. The time has come for the Church to re-imagine itself so that the new wine of Vatican II and post-conciliar developments can begin to flow. If the Church is to address the ethical deficit that now exists in society, if it is to fill the spiritual vacuum that is all around, and if it is to transform the increasing levels of religious apathy, then it will need to operate out of a new imagination.

Dermot A. Lane

MUSEUM or garden? When Pope John called the Second Vatican Council, he confided to a friend that his task was that of launching a big and heavy ship. 'Another,' he said prophetically 'will have the task of taking it out to sea'.

My generation saw that as our task and privilege and we were encouraged in that belief. One of our professors, Kevin McNamara, later Archbishop of Dublin, helped us to tease out the implications of a new and exciting theology of Church - the need to cherish difference, to unpack the richness of diversity, to keep an eye out for the signs of the times and the movement of God's Spirit emanating from the most unexpected places.

We gulped it all down, avidly, the milk of Mother Church. Thirty years later I look back with huge disappointment and anger. Tread softly for you tread on my dreams. We were, in effect, deceived. We bought the line. A theological disenfranchisement took place as the new orthodoxy was redefined as heresy in three decades.

When I see the tide of Vatican II being rolled back systematically, when I see a benign and sycophantic leadership bowing to the whims of Vatican bureaucrats who haven't a clue about what it means to live in the modern world I long for leaders, like the late Cardinal Leon Suenens of Belgium, with the vision and the courage to lead us out of the darkness of this time.

When I see safe men being appointed as bishops I long for a confident and charismatic leader who isn't afraid to live on the edge or to put out his or her stall in the marketplace of ideas, someone with the passion and expertise to preach the gospel truth without qualifying every second word out of existence.

When I see priests broken as human beings through isolation and loneliness I want someone with authority and credibility to say that it needn't be this way.

When I see lay (that derogatory term) people patronised by church structures that are out of tune with the needs of the Christian community and the democratic and collaborative ethos of our time, I long for someone to name the way the baptised are systematically disenfranchised in their own church.

When I see people wishing the church well, wanting the church to do well, pleading for a church with which their children can connect, I want someone to help us believe that our response to that need is more than a public relations exercise to keep the faithful happy.

When I see loyalty to a person or an institution being valued more highly than the long-term needs of the church, I long for someone to explain that loving the church is not the preserve of those who always agree with the status quo.

When I see women walk away from the church in frustration at the way they are patronised and demeaned by the institution, I long for someone to hold out some hope for some iota of movement in the direction of justice and reason.

When I see the *Code of Canon Law* or *The Catechism of the Catholic Church* or the Pope being quoted more often than Sacred Scripture, I wonder what agenda that priority is designed to serve.

When I see bishops giving more attention to the lunatic fringe with their visions and their absurd messages purportedly from Our Lady, I long for a leader who will confront this gobbledygook once and for all in the name of a gospel truth and a theologically defensible mariology.

When I sense careerists responding to whatever way the wind is blowing and blending with the wallpaper of whatever room they happen to be in at the time, I want to protest against the ethos of politicking that is surely not what God intended for his Church.

When I hear church-people getting themselves into a twist about the minutiae of sexual morality, I long for someone to say that we should close our churches until we respect and respond to the needs of hundreds of Traveller children living in appalling conditions on the side of the road.

When I hear my fellow-priests talk about the disservice mandatory celibacy is doing to the Church throughout the world, I long for someone to have the courage to name that difficult truth in Ireland. Not just to speak about it *sotto voce* when the bishop has left the room or the brandy has been consumed.

Exaggerated? Yes, to make a point. But is anyone listening anymore? While different emphases emerge, there is a basic struggle going on for the soul of the Church - between those who want an open, accountable, participatory Church that finds its rationale in the Vatican II documents and in the compulsions of our people, and those who have turned the wagons into a Tridentine circle.

For Vatican II afficionados, the temptation is to throw the ball away and leave the field. But that is a counsel of despair. Better not to concede the middle ground, to argue the toss rather than drift or be pushed to the margins. Especially now. For suddenly the dense and stifling air of Trent has cleared a little with the difficult truth that the wonderful past seems less impressive as the media lift stone after reluctant stone and disturb a noxious undergrowth.

Because this is a time of hope, purification, kenosis. Opportunity, we're often told by the despairing, is the other side of crisis. Mary Robinson's secular Ireland speaks a language of partnership and collaboration and the oppressive structures of a past age are thrown into embarrassing relief. The three modern sisters – Accountability, Openness and Transparency – are discomfiting and unwelcome visitors for the Church, apart from the occasional public relations gloss when Mother Necessity demands it. Meanwhile, the 'hungry sheep' look up, are patronised, not fed, and are departing for more amenable pastures. That great beast clericalism still dominates the landscape but its days are numbered. The old Church is dying. The museum is falling down and much remains to be done in the garden.

That amenable truth is sensed rather than evident. A Church ostensibly based on the truth finds itself not believed by its own people and its leaders don't know what to do. In a dead forest fires spontaneously break out and are extinguished with growing desperation. Instead of letting the fires burn out so that the forest can renew itself naturally, energy and resources are expended in a fruitless effort to stay the inevitable.

The difficulty is that we seem to have lost the ability to examine analytically issues of importance and draw considered and credible conclusions, without obfuscating the whole exercise in silly piety and unwarranted optimism. We have lost too the ability to close the gap that is now obvious between what the Church says and what people believe and do. It is not just that the authority of bishops and priests has declined significantly; nor is it that the clerical world and its seeming esoteric concerns are of no compelling interest to our people; it is that in general terms bishops and priests seem to have little notion of how out of sync we are with the compulsions of ordinary life. In a world that presumes accountability and openness, we do jigs and reels about how every structure of importance is 'merely consultative' and we wonder why people look at us in dismay and walk away.

In a world where ability and performance presume responsibility, we invest the incompetent and the inarticulate with authority. In a world that builds into its institutions an effective self-critical mechanism, we dismiss as disloyal malcontents anyone who wants to name the truth. In a world where effective leadership has to do with clueing into the compulsions in people's lives we end up, like hardline unionists, saying 'No' to everything because we push it through the prism of a clerical mind. The way, for example, we demonise the compulsions of our times.

Secularism, that convenient excuse for the decline of religion, is simply a by-product of the times we live in. It's just a fact of life. It emerges not from a lack of a spiritual sense but from scientific, economic and technological advances. Once we prayed for good weather: now we watch the weather forecast. We know more so we have less in the tray marked, 'Mysteries of

Life'. That's just the way it is. It doesn't make us less religious, or more sinful, just that we're living in a different world.

Materialism may be not so much a sin as another fact of life in a developed economy. Are we less religious because cars have replaced bicycles? Or tractors have replaced the hand-plough? Or because people can afford to go on holidays? Or because we have so many labour-saving devices? Again, materialism isn't something that of itself makes us less religious. People have more but surely not so much more that it compromises their sense of God.

Individualism is seen as a product of secularism and materialism killing community and birthing an obsession with our own lives. But is that true? Individualism is often no more than a celebration of the uniqueness of the individual. God created every one of us as unique individuals, down to our unique finger-prints. Surely the world is right to rejoice in that.

And what is dismissed as *relativism* is a new, questioning freedom, resistant to unelected authority and suspicious of organised religion, a freedom that is intent on placing in context the more complex and intractable bits of life and bringing to bear on them the primacy of individual conscience.

Unpack what passes for intelligent comment and one bishop's *materialism* can become parents' concern for their children, *secularism* can mean a firm grasp of the compulsions of the surrounding world, *relativism* can mean a necessary sense of how realities impinge on one another and *individualism* can be no more than encouraging the varied plants of John XXIII's garden.

What we don't seem to be able to fathom is how so much has changed so quickly. Who thought that the museum would have crumbled so quickly? We got glimpses of it, of course. Like when the Irish bishops issued a statement in the run-up to the last divorce referendum and we sensed the damage the Irish bishops' statement did to the 'No' cause?

People have told me that their proposed 'No' vote was, at the very least, put in jeopardy by the rigidity and insensitivity they perceived in the bishops' statement. Others sought but couldn't find in the statement the erstwhile clear distinction between law and morality or a clear statement that, in line with the Decree on Religious Liberty, Catholics could in good conscience vote 'Yes'. Others wondered why in a statement from spiritual leaders there was so much sociology and so little Scripture.

For some at least the unwarranted confidence of the bishops and the absolute conviction with which they expressed their view was the final nail in the coffin of their allegiance to the Church. It was for them a declaration that life was black and white when to them everything seemed forty shades of grey. It had the clarity of a text-book definition when what they experienced was the messiness of life. It was about pretending that the vast complexity of life could be effortlessly flattened out into clear categories of right and wrong. For them it seemed almost a last anthem for a disappearing world.

So what do we do? Clearly we need some forum in the Irish Church – possibly diocesan synods – that would create an authentic listening opportunity for our leaders as well as a healing of the hurts of our people. To ensure that such would be taken seriously, we first need to cultivate the ground properly. That would involve some kind of declaration of intent that has the merit of measuring the seriousness of that intent. For too long we have, like De Valera draining the Shannon before every election, dealt too often the false joker of aspiration. The trumpeting of the Code of Canon Law didn't extend to implementing some of its requirements like Parish Pastoral Councils, Diocesan Pastoral Councils and so forth. Even at one stage there was a statement that every

parish in Ireland was going to have a Liturgy Group! We
were told what the Pope was saying, what the bishops
were going to do, what the clergy would like to see
happening, what the Law of the Church required and
even though there was an admirable at-oneness about
what could happen in theory, little was happening in
practice. Time after time we brought our people to the
edge of the water and we sent them away thirsty. As a
result the problem now is that they won't heed us
anymore. A first challenge we have to overcome is: how
can we re-establish the trust of the people?

The second is a declaration that recognises the sins of
the past. Not something that comes off a public relations
agenda, not something that is by way of reluctant
concession but a sense that the pain has been felt and the
cry has been heard. You don't often get that sense when
bishops talk. Some years ago now Helena O'Donoghue -
in the wake of a moving and grim documentary *The
Magdalen Laundry* on the experiences of unmarried
mothers in an institution run by Mercy Sisters -
apologised on radio to all who had suffered in this and
other institutions at the hands of the nuns. I mused at the
time, in *Intercom*, an in-house priests' magazine, as to
when a bishop would go on *The Late Late Show*,
Ireland's largest congregation, and apologise to the Irish
people for the sins of the clerical Church. At the time my
suggestion was derided as ridiculous. Now it almost
seems that every time a bishop sees a microphone they
are rushing to it to add their tuppenceworth of apology.
All well and good but you sense that the words are being
spoken but that they carry no weight.

Another concern is to communicate a sense of
urgency in our approach. While it is important to get
things right rather than to do things quickly, there comes
a point at which telling people that there is a committee
sitting on something is simply an admission of failure.
That may be vaguely tolerable for the ICEL committee

who have been working on a revision of the liturgical texts for years but at this point issues as explosive as, say, the sexual abuse of children by clergy deserve a more sensitive, more upfront and rapid response. Those taking the long and historic view of Church affairs may be able to place this traditional laid back philosophy in context but the non-clerical world won't grant such indulgence.

Another concern is to convince lay people that clergy are more self-aware and recognise the need to critique their work. This is a sour sweet to suck on. Some years ago Fr Ray Brady in *The Furrow* suggested that the dark side of priesthood should be investigated. In more confident times, he wasn't thanked for his remarks and was subsequently savaged by his fellow-priests in the pages of *The Anglo-Celt*. I could empathise with his predicament. We know now, even if it wasn't quite as evident then, that loyalty to the clerical brotherhood demands a bit more than cheering indiscriminately from the sidelines especially when such cheering drowns out the quiet voices of question and reason that struggle to be heard. Independent spirits in the Church, rather than being dismissed as mavericks, should be unambiguously cherished.

A corollary to self-critique is an acknowledgement that an ethos of accountability and participation is a *sine qua non* for the Church in the future. This is no longer an option to be discussed. It is simply a measure of trust and without it there will be no trust. There's no point in announcing another set of guidelines within which priests or parishes are expected to operate unless, within a reasonable time-frame, it begins to happen.

There is, as well, a feminist deficit the Church has to make up. Language, a certain emotional illiteracy, an inability to contextualise the hurt, are merely part of the mountain that a male church has to climb. The emphasis surely is on active and participatory listening if that is not simply beyond us. What presents as sweet reasonableness to clerical ears can be accurately construed as sexist, and even exclusive, if not arrogant.

A recognition that we have for centuries operated out of an almost exclusively male wisdom, that our theology and tradition have descended through a genetically one-sided avenue, that the limitations of patriarchy are obvious to all, are no more than necessary parameters for starting a debate.

But the big question remains: how can we get it into our heads that a sea-change has taken place, that things will never be the same again, that the boundaries have permanently shifted, that the clerical perspective is way off beam and that the sands of time are simply running out?

CHAPTER THREE
Change just is

We run faster and faster trying to catch up with the past which we have irretrievably lost.

F. Scott Fitzgerald

THIRTY years ago, when I was ordained, the July '73 issue of *The Furrow* had articles on Teresa of Avila, Dom Marmion and *New Ways in Christology*, two catechetical reports, the inevitable homilies, a few worried letters about *Charismatic Renewal and Grace* and a report on *Co-Responsibility and the Clergy*. And among the names: Gerry McGarry, Kevin McNamara, James Mackey, James Good, C.M. Gray-Stack and Fr Donal O'Lehane from Shannonbridge.

Thirty years on, the issue of April 2003 has an article on *Caring for Clergy Offenders* (child sexual abuse), an opinion piece about a *Church with Imagination,* a featured review of Irish Catholicism - The Undoing of a Culture, another review of a book by the scientist and atheist Richard Dawkins and an article on covetousness.

I furnish what may present as gratuitous detail because it places a marker, a context for the two worlds we now uncomfortably straddle, the Church of the nineteenth century and the Church *for* the twenty-first, loyalty to the food of our youth coupled with a growing sense of its nutritional limitations.

The two worlds that thirty years ago I sought to straddle (if you'll pardon the indelicate anatomical allusion) have not produced a workable synthesis. On the one hand is the nineteenth century Church: traditional devotions, catechism answers, a spirituality of acceptance, a morality without compromise, a dogma without development, a discipline that is austere and based on sacrifice, a wisdom that is based on an impoverished understanding of tradition, a pastoral practice that is based on being told what to do, a liturgy with Latin hymns and incense, priests with black suits and Roman collars, nuns with veils, laypeople with certainty written all over them.

On the other hand is the Church for the twentieth century first century: liturgies that connect with the experience of life today, a spirituality that challenges, a morality written not just out of the head but with echoes in the heart, a dogma that listens, a discipline that understands what we're made of and what we can be, a wisdom based not just on tradition but on the life-enhancing insights of the present time, priests and nuns and laypeople who relate as human beings because they can feel the frets and the joys and the questions that life throws up.

At present we're caught between the two worlds represented above. Somewhere between the world of

Eamon de Valera and that of Mary Robinson, between those who look back on a world where piety, permanence and simplicity were the norm and those who look forward to the opportunities and the challenges that lie ahead. De Valera represents where we were: Robinson where we'd like to be.

This interregnum is a crucial time and history will not be kind to those who lose their nerve. My own conviction is that while we thank God for the faith and the richness of the past, the time has come to stop looking back at the bright and rosy summers of yesteryear and to plan for the increasing worrisome future. My fear is that because we insist on not planning, because we pander to those who want to bring us back to the nineteenth century, because we insist on proposing yesterday's answers to today's questions, we are losing the battle for the faith and practice of the people.

This time is crucial and we need to use it now. We need to plan, to devise strategies, to shape the Church of the future. It will be a more person-centred Church, a more user-friendly and accountable Church, above all, a layperson's Church. It will be about what the heart is saying as well as the head, what women know as well as what men say, the promise as well as the past. The old world is gone and there is a brave new Church waiting to be born. So the focus, as Pope John Paul reminds us and as we need to remind his often uncritical admirers, is on 'a sense of urgency'. Prudence will in retrospect seem a poor companion.

Some will ask: why change a successful formula? If, in rural areas, fifty to sixty per cent of people are still going to Church, and if the percentage is going down a point or two, so what? That was the statistic in one part of Canada some years ago and now it's down to 15%. But, people said, *that's Canada, Canada isn't Ireland.* Then in parts of Dublin it went down to 14%. *But that's Dublin*, they said, *that isn't the country.* So when it's 14%

in Roscommon, will they be saying, *"But that's Roscommon, this is Mayo"*? This kind of denial is difficult to understand. We have no problem accepting that if in economic matters, New York gets a wheeze, London gets a chill and Ireland gets pneumonia. Yet we dismiss out of hand the mountains of growing evidence to substantiate a similar pattern in matters pastoral.

Of course, it's one thing to know the road to take; it's quite a different matter to be able to make the journey. The unpalatable truth is that the one group - the church clerical - which we imagined could facilitate and nurture this new Church, lacks the confidence to connect with it and the ability to do it. If the museum is falling down on the heads of those who for years have been responsible for its maintenance, then it seems logical to presume that we need outside help.

Thirty years ago, I was sitting in the barque of Peter at the mouth of a harbour. Those who prepared me for the voyage had over the seminary years encouraged me to believe that on ordination I would be joining a craft that would turn away from the safety of the harbour and face the strains and currents of the rising tide. I wasn't promised, as the song says, a rose garden. I could feel the cold winds of change. I knew the risks I was taking. Indeed some of the crew were already leaving. But I bought the seriousness of the intent. After all, the captain kept talking in glowing terms about the Council that fired my decision. This was no *Yes, Minister* scenario where the public relations snuff had no substance to it. This was to be the great adventure, and I was happy, indeed privileged, to be part of it.

Thirty years on the anger at the deceit has abated somewhat and I, and many like me, find ourselves paddling the murky waters of regret and cynicism. Because thirty years on, the captain has changed his mind, the vessel is listing, some of the first-mates have gone over the side and we're heading back to the shore.

The indicators are that we won't make it. Most of the crew are below deck celebrating a golden jubilee and pining for the good old days. A few sad souls are still talking into the wind about God writing straight with crooked lines. A few more still believe that God in his humourous way is indicating that our only hope is to head once more for the Seven Seas and renew acquaintance with those old characters 'Co-responsibility' and 'Collegiality' and their friends. The dream has faded but the possibilities remain.

Part of the difficulty with accepting change is that for the Church the best time is always yesterday. It's difficult not to look back with something approaching nostalgia at what we imagine was a Golden Age. The truth is, of course, that there was never a Golden Age. As we grow older or more insecure, we force the varied inconveniences of life through the great sieve of memory. Eventually, everything (it seems) used to be better.

The Corpus Christi processions, the Men's Sodality, the Children of Mary, women in hats, Mass in Latin, fish on Friday . . . anthems of another age suddenly hug the memory and transport us back to a simpler and more enduring life. But even though it is no more than a generation ago, such epiphanies of certainty and stability seem curiously out of tune with the reason and convenience of the modern age.

Yet it's easy to understand the temptation to pull back, to imagine that we can reinvent the past or at least visit it occasionally. In the country of memory we imagine we see conviction rather than opinion, community rather than individualism, care instead of independence, the WE principle instead of the ME solution. Or at least, that may be how it appears. The grim truth is found somewhere between the remembered and the imagined.

But the truth, grim or otherwise, is that the very pulse of change is a constant in the makeup of our time. The old world is dying or has died and we have to cope with a

new and difficult birth. While age and wisdom pine for
stability and certainty, youth and passion seek more
tangible goals. Dizzying developments in technology,
biology, communications and the varied developments of
our time compound the general feeling of being
passengers on a locomotive careering out of control
while vague figures in the distance wave goodbye to us.

It is difficult to appreciate the sea-change that has
taken place. Even at everyday level. Imagine a world
without frozen foods, plastics, contact lenses,
photocopiers, credit cards, word processors, the
contraceptive pill, colour television, biros, pizzas, videos,
dishwashers, electricity. Imagine alongside it a world of
wind-up telephones, steam radio, Ovaltine, Joe Linnane's
Question Time, porridge, liquid of Paraffin, cars with no
heaters and marrowfat peas.

Older people like myself remember a time when
things were so quaint that people actually got married
before they lived together, when *a meaningful
relationship* meant getting on well with your cousins,
when *fast food* was what you ate during Lent, divorce
was something that happened to film stars, *grass* was
something you mowed, *coke* was a cold drink and *AIDS*
were for those with hearing difficulties.

The pace of change is so unrelenting that nostalgia for
a return to the simplicity and the stability of the past is a
form of death-wish. We can no more peel back the
decades than we can push back the proverbial toothpaste
into the tube. To attempt it would be senseless and
defeatist.

This doesn't mean compromising on what we believe
but it does mean pushing what we believe through the
prism of life today. For instance, it is no longer sufficient
that someone in authority simply hands down an official
wisdom. Unless it is capable of being translated in such a
way that it resonates with the lived experience of those
for whom it is intended, it is perceived not just as

incomprehensible or irrelevant but as a distancing factor in terms of the Church. Unless teaching on marriage, for instance, echoes the lived experience of Christian married couples today, it may have the effect of alienating rather than affirming.

The litmus test of what is acceptable, in this as in other areas, is whether something makes sense 'to me now'. This is not to suggest that everything can be minimalised to what makes sense *now* but simply to say that what we believe has to be argued for in the great marketplace of ideas today. Saying, 'It's true because I say it's true', is a recipe for alienation.

The truth is that things have changed. The controlled, self-sufficient world that produced family, food, values, marriage partners, entertainment and religion has disappeared. The world is smaller; mobility has increased dramatically; the communications revolution has opened up a volcano of ideas fighting for a soundbyte of our attention. Very few remember who Dominic Savio was but everyone knows Michael Jackson; Padraic Pearse is hardly mentioned anymore but Jack Charlton became a national hero; bishops almost have to apologise for opening their mouths but Eamon Dunphy is a guru. It's not what podium you happen to stand on anymore but whether you make sense.

We live in a culture that is in a continual state of flux. Individualism is becoming the ethos of the day; participation in decision-making that affects the individual is regarded as a personal right not an institutional concession; moral relativism is the tenor of our time, what is right is what is right 'for me'.

So we are left with the difficult questions: How can a received wisdom live with that kind of society? How can a sense of community responsibility be preserved in a world of rampant individualism? How can we find a faith and a liturgy that connects with the world we live in?

Part of the answer surely must be that we have to

leave aside many of the old ways. The priest will have to divest himself of the trappings of power, real or imaginary; lay people will have to assume greater responsibility for the Church we tell them is theirs; the agenda of the young will have to be brought centre-stage; the old rituals and rubrics of life will have to be submitted to the chill winds of reason and relevance. Change has not so much to be endured as to be accepted and embraced.

All of this has been said before. And we have fiddled with the edges. But the middle ground that we thought would always hold firm is breaking up under our feet. The religious consensus that we have so uncritically enjoyed for so long is disappearing and we need new insights, different skills, a greater sense of urgency. We need a courage that will permit failure, a strength that can endure, a Church that will be radically different from what we are now. The time for tinkering around with amenable strategies is over.

Change is a difficult steed to ride. Only the masochistic enjoy skiing on a landslide. The old world is dying but very few seem happy, as local papers invariably have it, 'to officiate at the obsequies'. In other dispensations grief counsellors advise that all good things must come to an end, man that is born of woman hath but a short time to live, to everything there is a season, dust to dust, ashes to ashes and so forth. But back in the real world, change is not a pill to be popped unthinkingly.

Whether we can take the tide of change is another question. Old institutions and old habits die hard. I am reminded of a story told by Donald Schon in his 1970 Reith Lectures about attempts to introduce modern technology into an artillery regiment in the British Army. The regiment was equipped with new rapid-fire guns deployed on a motorised carrier but it was found that the regiment's rate of fire in field conditions was much lower than anticipated. A time-and-motion study revealed that at a certain point in the firing cycle one soldier would stand motionless at a short distance from the others. When this apparently illogical practice was put to the commanding officer, he replied that the soldier was 'holding the horses, old boy'.

The story nicely illustrates the pathological resistance to change in great institutions, the difficulty of changing not just ways of working but a complete mind-set. For just as the army's procedures for controlling their horses during fire outlived the switch to motorised technology, so too many of the supposedly immutable rites, rituals and practices of the Church will in future years be recalled with the same wry incredulity.

Some will remember a time when there were only male priests; when Parish Pastoral Councils didn't actually exist or did exist in fact but not in reality; when there was only private Confession; when bishops were chosen by a Vatican Congregation and not by the people and priests of their own diocese; when priests were appointed by the bishop and not on the recommendation of the people; even as far back as when priests were all celibate. And bishops and their husbands will regale their grandchildren with would-you-believe-it stories from the dark ages of the Church.

In a happier age, collegiality will be a basic tenet of faith and praxis. The principle of subsidiarity (whereby a larger body is not allowed subvert the role or function of a smaller group) will be given a central role in determining appropriate functions of different bodies. The present 'political' model of Church, whereby the focus is on control and power, will be balanced by an emphasis on the 'communion' model whereby the diversity of gifts will be given free expression. The centralising role of the Curia will be limited and authority expressed more through the local (diocesan) Church.

Part of the difficulty is that we tend to smile at such naivety. Few appreciate the pace of change. Yet it's an incontestable truth of our time that with developments in technology and information superhighways, change is an unstoppable train careering irresistibly into an uncertain future. We can't plan its course anymore than we can stunt its progress. We either stay with it or we can become like the Amish, building a religious ghetto of interest only to ourselves and the occasional passing tourist.

And even though it's understandable that we often fail to appreciate and acknowledge the pace of change, it's devastating to hear church leaders misreading the signs of the times to such an extent that they imagine that change can be managed, that they believe that the storms will pass and the self-contained little clerical world that oppresses and stunts the Church will again set confident sail in more tranquil waters. That day is well and truly gone and all the episcopal edicts under the sun, all the black suits in all the drapery shops of the world, all the plugging of larger and larger leaks in the great dam of modern life and all the Pope's men won't put it back together again.

The operative emblem for this change is that of Seamus Heaney as a young child watching the delicate ripples form on the surface of a bucket of water in the scullery as a train sped past in the distance. No matter how we try to shutter out the world, in a quiet Derry townland or in the Church, the reverberations break through. The churchquake, as someone described it, is moving the ground under our feet and we can no more hold the past than we can stay the world around us.

'The past,' one Angelo Roncalli (later Pope John XXIII) said in 1933, 'will never return.' At the beginning of a new century, would that we could only believe it? 'We run faster and faster' wrote F. Scott Fitzgerald 'trying to catch up with the past which we have irretrievably lost.' It is a counsel of despair. Like latterday Quixotes, we tilt at the great windmills of 'materialism', 'individualism', 'selfism', and imagine them as a pernicious philosophy rather than as, at best, the struggle for freedom after an age of oppressive control or, at worst, the inevitable shadow side of human nature.

Yet, as a church, we often rage against the spirit of the age we live in, achieving no more than managing to lose our way in the slipstream of history. We stand on the shore blustering against the incoming tide of the modern world and we wonder why the water has reached our knees. We hold forth against contraception, divorce and abortion and we suddenly realise that no one is listening to us anymore.

And worse still we imagine that this negative and self-defeating approach is a credible strategy. You'd imagine that it didn't run counter to what we believe about Incarnation and Mission. You'd imagine that the Berlin Wall had never fallen, that the Soviet Union was still going strong, that Havel's Velvet Revolution had never taken place, that the 'end of history' as we know it was not at hand. You'd imagine that as a Church we were successfully communicating with the teenage generation, that we had linked into the concerns and compulsions of young married people, that we were able to communicate with the 'movers and shakers' in our society, that those who struggle through the small hours of belief find in us a perceptive and credible empathy. You'd imagine that we were finding a way of helping people cope with the alienation and bleakness of modern life, when the truth is that we don't even know the words to use. We're not even at the pictures. And, worse still, we don't even know it.

A new Church struggles to be born. It will be a difficult birth as we try to cope with the death that precedes it. Like any grieving it will be difficult to manage as it goes through the different stages of denial, anger, depression and acceptance. Some are still in denial, hoping against hope that somehow it's all going to go away. Others are angry that the death took place at all.

Others again in deep depression because the world has fallen apart and they have no other world to live in. And still others searching for the space to accept that a wisdom that served the Church for so long has so little to say to us now.

So we pine for the rituals that sustained us for many generations, though maybe not as many as we sometimes imagine. We struggle to leave behind the superfluous accretions of the centuries that weigh us down and inhibit our growth. We worry about the decline in vocations as the priesthood is restructured. We worry about the demise of religious congregations as we struggle to come to terms with the reality of a lay-driven Church.

And yet the Church, as we know it, *is* dying. And without death, there is no new life. But just as God provides in every generation for his Church, God will raise up leaders of energy, ability and imagination, women and men who will help us shed the tired accumulations of the past and focus anew on the effort to know, love and serve the God of Jesus Christ. And as surely as night follows day, a new and vibrant Church will rise from the dead forests of the past, a seedling sprouting new shoots of life and growth. And those who can't live with the change will be out there somewhere on the margin explaining to everyone that someone has to hold the horses.

Change comes whether we wish it or not. The great swell of life's tide doesn't decide to ebb because we'd prefer if it did, thank you very much, or because someone passes a resolution or issues a diktat. Change just is. Accepting that fact is a big step into a very different future and towards a very different Church.

CHAPTER FOUR

Keeping reality at bay

In an age when we have the most educated laity that the Church has ever had, they have no more influence on ecclesiastical decisions than their peasant predecessors; and within dioceses and parishes collaborative ministries have foundered on the inability of clerical bureaucrats to share power.

James O'Connell

WHILE it's only in retrospect that we designate an exceptional period of history as a 'Golden Age', surely such a case can be made for the present time. Our Celtic Tiger economy, though now taking a breather, has created undreamt of opportunities; there's renewed hope that the intractable Northern problem is moving towards resolution; Irish Nobel prizewinners in literature and world champions in sport are part of the currency of our time; our participation in Europe has given us a renewed confidence in ourselves; our President, representing our growing confidence as a people, has raised our stock in the world; and there's a bounce in the national step. Suddenly Ireland, in Harold MacMillan's phrase, never had it so good.

But pan the camera to the Irish Church and the colour begins to fade and the picture begins to wobble until it settles into fuzzy grey. Morale is low, decline is evident, ennui is the prevailing mood and the lack of confidence is palpable. It is one of the peculiar anomalies of our time that in a society where everything seems to be moving into the Premier League, the Church seems to have been relegated to the furthest reaches of the Vauxhall Conference.

Once upon a time as priests we felt we were breaking new ground; we were captains of our own ships; we spoke a language of possibility and promise. Now we till the same patch of exhausted ground; the craft is listing dangerously; we become marginal to the forces that matter and we find ourselves looking on at a distance - powerless, irrelevant, imploding. The Church focus is hopelessly narrowing while the rest of society is looking out confidently to the wider world. It is as if we are again being defined, as clergy and as a Church, by the grey image of a Corpus Christi procession of the Fifties, which in our present technicolour world, represents decline and irrelevance.

The parameters of influence have shifted dramatically. Irish society has danced to our jig for so long that we now find it difficult to get used to our new peripheral status of pulling the curtains while others take the centre of the stage. Indeed we can retain a certain fiction that we still matter, that in the corridors of power we still carry some weight.

This fantasy can sometimes have unintended comic consequences. At a clerical gathering, the discussion turned to the fairly recent decision of the Supreme Court that a provision in the Employment Equality Act which allows employers in religious institutions to discriminate in order to maintain a religious ethos was constitutional. With the comfortable benefit of hindsight, the consensus at the meeting was that the Supreme Court really had no alternative. After all, hadn't the Church created the educational system? Hadn't we a certain proprietorial interest in the whole business and if we withdrew from it, wouldn't it collapse like a house of cards? Similarly, this novelty of appointing mere lay people as Chairpersons of Boards of Management of primary schools was, legend had it, doomed to failure because, unlike the clergy, laypeople were presumed not to have the experience or the background of managing education. The fact that the ability of many of those who encouraged this nonsense just about extended to the managerial equivalent of collecting eggs from a hen-house once a day hardly seemed to matter. What mattered was the fiction that we could still hack it. That we still *matter*.

Another embarrassing example of the same fiction is the occasional outburst of arrogance from churchmen who, convinced that what the Church and by extension society needs is *strong leadership*, proceed to patronise and insult the wisdom, intelligence and common sense of the generality of people. The grotesque spectacle of some clerical maverick laying down the law on some peripheral issue and blithely unaware of the embarrassment and damage he's causing to the credibility and position of a reeling Church, is becoming part of a new media subculture. Naturally the media give the individual involved more than enough rope to hang himself. The common perception is that the Church, despite the PR gloss we have managed to put on things, will never learn the obvious lessons. We still believe that after all that has happened, everything is still the same.

This fiction not only convinces us that our present marginal status is a temporary setback and we will soon be called home from exile to take the reins of power and influence again, but it also renders us incapable of recognising the wisdom that the secular world has to offer to us. For instance the present or recent growth of Irish society is based on two factors: huge investment in education and in infrastructure. Could it be that there's a lesson there for the Church if we have the humility to learn it?

Part of the difficulty is our reluctance to buy into what's perceived as secular wisdom. We're different. We're not just another institution. God is with us. This excuses a radical re-assessment of practices and attitudes.

This creates its own unpromising sub-culture. For instance, in church circles, the most popular meeting is the one that arrests momentum (deciding why nothing can be done) not the one that facilitates it (deciding what and how something can be done), the meeting that is an end in itself rather than one that is in danger of transforming itself into a series. So the process is that decisions are made by a few and a wider representative group is then gathered to assent to them. And whenever groups gather with an open agenda (and without the final decision agreed beforehand), once the tide begins to flow in an unexpected direction, the official presider can suddenly discover that he has another meeting to attend. At a recent two-day gathering of priests, bets were taken by some of the participants on how long the bishop would attend. Even though the particular dates had been agreed beforehand to facilitate his diary, serious money changed hands when midway though the second day the discussions were becoming *interesting* and he discovered a meeting in Dublin he just had to attend.

So the rules that govern secular institutions are not perceived as applying to the Church. So priests are told to say their prayers as if somehow saying our prayers divests us of the responsibility of using our minds; lay people are told that their contribution is of a necessarily consultative nature; and someone retells the old story about good Pope John telling God to look after his Church because he was tired and was going to bed.

We end up becoming more and more separate from the wisdom and the vocabulary of our times as we allow a limited understanding of Tradition to paint us into a corner.

The history of Parish Pastoral Councils (PPCs) is a case in point. After the Second Vatican Council, PPCs appeared out of the fog of change and gradually disappeared again. The promulgation of the *New Code of Canon Law* and the publication of the Synod Document *Christifideles Laici* gave them added impetus but with little real effect. Almost forty years after the Council, few parishes have effective PPCs. There are two reasons for this. One is that, in church law, PPCs are of their nature consultative. This gives the priest a virtual veto on what can be discussed, what will be decided and in some cases whether they exist at all.

Thirty years ago, a percentage of people could ignore that limitation. Now most people find it patronising and offensive. Societies and organisations have become more democratic, more accountable and more professional and are used to taking group responsibility for difficult decisions and for large budgets. Credit unions, sporting organisations, hospice movements and many others are fuelled by an ethos of accountability and transparency and led by people of ability and commitment, used to the difficult business of a decision-making process that strives for real consensus. In effect, an exact model of what an effective, efficient, representative PPC should be. From time to time such people are elected to PPCs. Then when they attend a few meetings they realise that, in comparison to their work experience and to their involvement in similar non-religious activity, PPCs seem in effect a carry-over from a by-gone age, and they gradually drift away. This means that eventually PPCs are comprised of those who actually believe that *Father knows best*. We are drawing our representatives for PPCs from a diminishing constituency in terms of ability and commitment. The plain truth is that in today's world PPCs are not credible institutions.

That's not to say that an individual priest in a given set of circumstances cannot create an ethos of accountability and transparency and take on board the movers and shakers in his parish. It does happen. But rarely. And progressively PPCs are regarded as failed entities often with less status and demanding less expertise than membership of the local Agricultural Show Committee. Now, in the main, priests are happy with the sycophantic and gelded committees that create the fiction of Parish Pastoral Councils. The appropriate books have been written, diocesan committees to facilitate formation and development of PPCs have been in existence for years, and with a progressively less competent clergy the need was never more obvious. But in the thirty plus years since the Council, despite all the huffing and puffing, we have hardly moved in the direction of effective and efficient PPCs which are owned and respected by the celebrated People of God. Why is this?

One of the best kept secrets of the years since the Council has been the power of the clergy and the stranglehold they have on the church. In the early days of the Council, the word from Rome was that the days of the immovable Parish Priest were coming to an end. The phrase 'immovable PP' had its own internal logic. Priests were like huge wrecks at the mouth of a harbour. Every other sea-going vessel had to carefully negotiate around them. They rarely moved and when they did every drop in the ocean seemed to move with them in sympathy or in support. The conciliar wisdom was that the clerical wreck would be blasted out of the water and the barque of Peter, listing to one side, would balance again in the water and set full sail out into the deep. A new

infrastructure would emerge to give substance to this
new-found balance. Diocesan Pastoral Councils, Parish
Pastoral Councils, Finance Committees and other worthy
notions would place the role of the priest in a more
pastoral perspective. The excitement and the energy
released by the Council and the new-found authority of
the local bishop confirmed the sense that change would
happen or be eased through. The theory was impressive
but it didn't allow for the virtual stranglehold the priest
had on the church.

In theory, Vatican II saw an increase in the status of
bishops, an advance in the role of the laity and a
consequent diminution in the power of the priest. In
practice, it didn't work out quite like that. What was
forgotten in the excitement was how central and
dominant was the role of the priest. And, like the
Unionists and others who see the world drifting away
from them, the easiest thing for priests to say was, 'No'.
A huge blocking exercise took place. The few bishops
who were convinced of the wisdom of the Council
cajoled and persuaded and arm-twisted and eventually
retreated exhausted to the margins, edging away from a
direct confrontation with their priests. Without the local
man on the ground buying and owning the new wisdom,
no movement could or would take place.

Eventually everyone recognised the importance of the
priest in the whole endeavour. Not least the priests
themselves. Like refugees from a religious version of *Yes
Minister*, priests up and down the golf courses of the
country decided what would or would not work, what
might work in some other place but not here, what might
work some other time but not under the current
circumstances. And, in extreme circumstances,
recognising the restoration ethos emanating from Rome
and the papacy of John Paul II, priests wondered out loud
whether there might be a gap between what a local
bishop wanted and what was perceived to be the opinion

of the Pope in Rome. And even though bishops (as is now their wont) prefaced their remarks with a string of quotations from the Holy Father, even though the pews started to empty, even though a variety of vessels took to the surrounding seas, the wreck remained at the mouth of the harbour with its ageing occupants clinging desperately to it.

In short, in the almost forty years since the Council, priests have effectively operated a blocking mechanism to the emergence of a more effective infrastructure for the church at local level. The reaction of the bishops has been in the main to accept the reality of a priests' veto. Defeated by priests in a series of skirmishes and convinced of their own inability to dictate progress, bishops have simply lost their nerve. Those who are not committed to the thrust of the Second Vatican Council or can't see what's happening around them are more than content to let things be; those who are committed are reduced to a peripheral and aspirational role and the vague hope that they can achieve some progress by stealth.

Even though nothing stands still and the flood of history, according to Auden (in an untypical mixed metaphor), held one moment, burns the hand, bishops are not prepared, or are unable, to implement the thrust of the Council for an infrastructure that would serve the Church into the future. It follows then that the logic of the workplace and the wisdom of our time are conveniently or necessarily set aside. We lapse into denial, creating a fiction of activity, holding meetings where nothing happens, ploughing the same half-acre with outdated implements and recycling a tired clerical wisdom. We try to convince ourselves that we are discerning and responding to the signs of the times by amassing reports, multiplying seminars and persuading ourselves into a vague optimism.

So what can be done? For one thing bishops need to own their own authority and confront the power of priests. The theological and pastoral role of bishops is clear. In the present dispensation we know who has to make the decisions. And tough decisions need to be made. If a priest accepts an appointment as PP or as CC, surely the purpose of the exercise is to do a job not to accept an honour, still less as a tribute to having lived a long and careful life. It follows then that the appointee should fulfil basic requirements: administer the sacraments, preach the Word of God, be involved in religious education programmes, have an effective PPC and, not least, demonstrate a basic efficiency in administering the parish and the parish plant. If the incumbent is seen to be negligent, it seems reasonable, in natural justice both to him and to the parish, to give him a less demanding role. However this rather obvious and reasonable solution is studiously avoided because it would mean confronting an unspoken clerical solidarity. The wreck at the mouth of the harbour has to remain undisturbed. Bishops are loth to confront their last remaining friends.

An antidote to this could be to replace the administrative functions of a PP (or a number of PPs in a cluster of parishes as suggested recently in Killaloe diocese) with a lay administrator. If the priest is incapable of or unwilling to organise his parish, then a lay administrator could be appointed to take charge of administration and to free the priest for a specifically priestly role. The lay administrator would work closely with the PPC and would be responsible to the bishop and the PPC for the overall administrative functioning of the parish: the work of the PPC, financial matters, maintenance of the parish plant. The appointing of lay administrators would free priests in busy parishes for real work, it would prepare for the time when the shortage of priests really begins to be felt, it would explode a few myths about the work-load of priests and in certain circumstances would have the effect of wonderfully concentrating the clerical mind, in that the gap between 'doing work' and 'being on duty' would be embarrassingly clear.

A second strand to this approach would be to give PPCs real, as distinct from imaginary, power and resource them accordingly. If bishops get upset when no Board of Management is elected in a primary school or when the BOMs fail to hold their requisite number of meetings, what message is it conveying to priests and people if there is no PPC in a parish or if it never meets and no one seems even slightly bothered? What message is it giving if a diocese has a priest looking after BOMs on behalf of the Department of Education but no one responsible for PPCs?

There is no reason why a PPC would not be in complete charge of the financial affairs of the parish, with officers signing cheques and being responsible for the efficient and constructive use of the people's money. There is no reason why PPCs should not be constituted in such a way as to overcome their merely consultative status and, while retaining their representative character, to maximise the possibility that a greater percentage of young adults (and an accordingly lesser percentage of older, more settled people who tend to grace every parish committee with their ineffective presence) would come forward to accept transparent and accountable responsibility for their parish community. I realise that this common sense approach might cause some difficulty in terms of the law of the Church but surely none that a few imaginative canon lawyers, if such there are, cannot overcome.

Another strand would be to name the real problems there are with PPCs. As we know there is a grey area in church affairs where bodies exist not to achieve anything in particular but to give the impression that something is happening. A former bishop in my own bailiwick annually inserted in the Irish Catholic Directory a list of people who had diocesan responsibilities for an impressive list of activities but the individuals involved often had no connection (and weren't expected to have any connection) with their respective titles. What mattered was not that anything happened over a range of important areas but that the impression was given that something was happening. In *Yes Minister*-speak, it would be called 'the Law of Inverse Relevance': the less you intend to do about something, the more you have to keep talking about it.

Likewise with PPCs, the ecclesiastical equivalent of draining the Shannon. What matters is that we continue to talk about them provided we make sure that we disengage the operation of our minds from the substance of what we say. The obvious truth is that more often than not PPCs are paper councils, lists of names thrown together which often have little existence apart from a file in the diocesan office. In most dioceses there are no formal formation programmes for members of PPCs (or for clergy) and where they do exist they are often used as a public relations exercise to impress the bishop. As part of a formally constituted diocesan body, I once helped to direct a formation course for a newly elected PPC. None of the three priests working in the parish attended and no meeting was held for a year and a half.

In his book *The Now and Future Church*, Eugene Kennedy said that managing change in the Church demanded, 'the exhausting pastoral art of encouraging change while holding it steady at the same time, something like giving a haircut to a drowsy lion.' Yet sometimes the lion has to be confronted, sometimes we cannot afford not to change. After all, what would be said of our politicians if the infrastructure and education that fuel the present booming economy had not been put in place over the last decade or so? What would our church be like now if during the last thirty years an effective infrastructure had been put in place? And what will we say of our leaders when the wheels really begin to come off in a few years time? More secrets waiting to be told, as R.S. Thomas wrote somewhere, when we are older and can stand the truth.

CHAPTER FIVE

The tyranny of clericalism

*The clerical culture in which I lived and worked seemed
as immutable as the Creed itself. It was neither
questioned nor critiqued. That such a culture tended to
keep priests emotionally immature and excessively
dependent on the approval of their superiors and
parishioners was yet to be understood.*

Donald Cozzens

SOME years ago Cardinal Cathal Daly made the point,
in an RTÉ interview, that part of the difficulty of
dealing with the IRA was that it was impossible to
communicate with them. They were in a time warp; they
had tunnel vision; they didn't seem to realise that time
had moved on and that Ireland had changed. They were
stuck with a particular mind-set that blocked
communication. In view of the irrational outrages to
which the Cardinal referred, it was impossible to quibble

with what he said. But, changing the subject fairly dramatically, it struck me at the time that perhaps the case could be made that, in a certain sense, his words were a metaphor for where we are as a church.

Because part of our problem as a church now is that while we have satisfactorily defined our church as 'the People of God' with all the inclusiveness that a common baptism entails, the truth is that at the heart of our church is a clerical culture, a debilitating mind-set that runs counter to our theology of Church.

'Clericalism' is about cherishing a mentality that believes that the clergy know best. The Church, despite the public relations spin we seem to need to put on things, will continue to be controlled by a secretive, exclusive, male, celibate, hierarchical and authoritarian elite. Around that exclusive club is a way of life that has to do with status, deference and privilege. Whenever a contrary wisdom presents itself (even a wisdom like that of the Second Vatican Council that demonstrably is from God) and the club feels itself attacked or under pressure the instinctive reaction is to protect the club, even at the cost of damaging the very message that the Church was founded to preach.

We saw more examples of this than we care to remember in the sex abuse scandals and the way church authorities sought to deal with them. The automatic reaction was to defend the institution, to downplay the seriousness of the damage done to children, to deny culpability, to try to protect the reputation of the Church, even at the cost of denying the very truth the Church is meant to serve. To our shame and humiliation as members of the Irish Catholic Church, we have witnessed in recent years the leaders of our church put the good of the institution (or the club) before the protection of children. We have watched in horror as our leaders, through their failure to own the gospel truth of Jesus Christ and their false loyalty to the institution of the

Church, further damaged through their actions the victims of clerical sex abuse. The question that begs to be asked is: how could decent and, we're assured, competent men find themselves in a situation where there was a yawning gap between the truth of Jesus Christ, which gives the whole church structure substance, and their economy with the truth in order to protect the institution?

Another example of the clerical club protecting its interests is the lip service the Church pays to the participation of women and the condescending attitude which often underpins it. Women are regularly invited to participate, are reassured of the valuable contribution they make but are in effect blocked from any role of significance. I remember once saying to a bishop that the best way to convince women that their participation in the Church was valued and appreciated was - even without conceding the possibility of ordination - to give them the fullest responsibilities within the present law of the Church. 'What do you mean?' he asked. 'Why not make women Cardinals?' I replied. (The rule that Cardinals must be priests only became part of the Code of Canon Law in 1916 so there is no point in pretending that some insuperable doctrinal argument exists which renders such an initiative untenable.) 'Or,' I went on 'women could be Chancellors of dioceses.' (There are as yet no women Chancellors in any Irish diocese.) 'And,' I continued, 'didn't Pope John Paul himself a few years ago, just before a visit to America, urge the Church to make use of the gifts of women in leadership positions? And don't we always make the point that ordination and authority are not necessarily linked?' My episcopal friend just smiled. He knew and I knew that all of that or even some of that simply isn't possible, as long as the clerical club continues to control the Church.

It isn't just from the evidence of the last decade or so that we realise how high a price the Church has paid for the culture of clericalism. We have had to live for centuries with an authority emanating from the narrow view of things that comes from exclusive maleness and celibacy. We have had to endure the arrogance of a clerical elite who believe that all wisdom is mediated through them, that they are in effect an exclusive conduit for the Holy Spirit. We have had to live with the rolling back of the teaching of the Second Vatican Council because it's focus on ideas like 'collegiality' and 'co-responsibility' threatened the powerbase of the clerical elite to decide and control everything. We have had to live with an understanding of the Church as divided into *Them* and *Us*: *Us* being those who are orthodox and conservative and defensive of the clerical club and *Them* being those disloyal, critical liberals who want to encourage dialogue and debate. We have had to accept the triumph of incompetent careerists who have successfully played the clerical game - wearing their black clothes, deferring to those who can influence appointments, addressing everyone by their formal ecclesiastical titles, sycophantly praising every utterance of their superiors, saying all the right things, cultivating all the right people and professing their utter orthodoxy on litmus-test issues of loyalty like celibacy, the ordination of women, *Humanae Vitae* and Marian devotion. We have had to witness the cringe-inducing nonsense of awarding empty honours to those members of the club who defer to the written and unwritten rules when no one had the courage to wish a plague on all their titles and privileges and fancy dress.

We have had to put up with the blather about some people being called *Reverend* and others being *Very Reverend* and others *Right Reverend*. And some even *Most Reverend*. What does all that matter in terms of the dignity and status that comes from our common baptism? We have Monsignors, Archdeacons, Vicars Forane, Chancellors, Precentors, Deans, Penitentiaries, Prebendaries, Canons and even Honorary Canons. Who are we trying to fool? As Leo Morahan wrote in *The Furrow* as far back as 1977,

> *'When a priest has played golf or whist with his colleague on Tuesday, how much more silly a game it is to send him a letter on Wednesday addressed to The Very Reverend Michael Canon O'Malley P.P., V.F. Who are we seeking to impress? The postman?'*

Rowan Williams, the new Archbishop of Canterbury, whom many believe is the great episcopal hope for reconnecting Christianity with modern culture, believes that the obsession of the clerical church with status has to be challenged. He said on television last year

> *The Anglican Church has bought very deeply into status. It's one of the most ambiguous elements in the whole of that culture - the concern with titles, the concern with the little differentiations, the different coloured buttons, as it were, the rosettes on the hat, as it used to be. And there have to be points where that gets challenged. There's something profoundly anti-Christian in all of that. It's about guarding position, about fencing yourself in. And that is not quite what the gospel is.*

Would that an Irish Roman Catholic bishop would challenge, what Christopher Morgan of *The Sunday Times* once called, 'the vanity of the over-promoted.'

That's what clericalism does. It tells us that it's better if our leaders make all the decisions; it tells us that the way bishops are appointed has nothing to do with anyone except those making the decisions; it tries to tell clergy that the will of the bishop is the will of God for them; it encourages priests to wear jet black clothes and Roman collars so that they can be easily distinguished as a separate caste; it tells lay people that they don't need to know what money is in what account or how it's spent as long as they keep paying; and, pathetically, it relives and recalls at exclusively clerical gatherings the perceived glories of the past when treasured customs based on privilege and elitism received due deference.

Clericalism is about living in a time warp. A different perspective, a different ethos, a different language. We talk to ourselves about issues in words that no one else understands. Just as the famous philosopher A. J. Ayer ended up questioning the existence of the chair on which he was sitting, we can be so mesmerised by the rubrics of a clerical world that we posit a self-contained existence full of answers to questions nobody is asking. When issues arise that have to do with the essential confusions of our times, we find ourselves parroting the set answers of a very different past rather that being prepared to stay with the difficult questions of the present. Part of this clerical mind-set has to do with imagining that we've seen it all before and talking into the ground any initiative that succeeds in getting through the sieve of clerical control. A few years ago, for example, in response to the Pope's request for a co-ordinated pastoral plan for Ireland, the Irish bishops launched a new initiative. It was an effort to establish what the present pastoral state of play was, to analyse where we were, to make decisions about where we wanted to go, to make things happen - and, if they didn't, to ask, why not? An expert was even employed to trudge from diocese to diocese and to meet with diocesan committees asked to attempt a pastoral audit of each diocese.

But the big question left hanging in the air was: if anything emerges from this huge project that might be worth doing, will anything happen? And even though the answer was in the affirmative, the clerical audience wasn't impressed. Or knew better. Nothing would happen because the clerical mind-set knows from long experience that things happen and only happen when the clergy agree to let them happen. Reports are compiled, initiatives suggested, strategies put in place, noises are made but the point of the exercise often is not that something should happen but that something should be seen to be happening.

A whole series of valuable and potentially effective initiatives have run aground on a tide of clerical opposition, or at least indifference. We know it all. We have been here before. The situation may not have been as problematic as now. The spoils of battle may not have been as important. The focus may not have been as clear. But every time something begins to happen, it is shot out of the water by a clerical torpedo powered by self-interest, oiled by cynicism, driven by fear.

Almost thirty years ago now, in 1974, the Irish bishops issued *Pastoral Guidelines* after a week long meeting in the Great Western Hotel in Mulranny in Co Mayo. The 'Mulranny' document was impressive in its scope and ambitious in its declared openness to change. The bishops set one clear priority

> *The main thrust of the Irish Church over the next five years should be the implementation of the principle of the involvement of the laity in the spiritual mission of the Church.*

The document went on to specify some recommendations. For example, Diocesan Pastoral Councils were, 'an excellent means towards bringing the life of the Church and the activity of the whole people of God within the diocese into greater conformity with the Gospel.' But there was no detailed plan, no one to drive the change, no accountability built into its implementation. If the same statement was being made today we'd be talking about the *organic* development of lay involvement which is another form of clergy-speak for something that might happen sometime in the future. Now, thirty years on, the Mulranny Guidelines (like the Great Western Hotel in Mulranny) are quaint and desolate memories, sometimes remembered as part of what we were, seldom recalled as part of what we might have been.

Yet despite all of that we're still talking up a new church. A recent example was Holy Thursday, 2003. An Irish bishop - Bill Murphy of Kerry - at the Chrism Mass in St Brendan's Cathedral in Killarney, told his assembled priests that he believes, 'a different and more exciting church is emerging, slowly and painfully' in Ireland. It was, he said, 'the kind of church envisaged by the Second Vatican Council, the kind of church needed in the twenty-first century: a consultative, participative, learning community, where there are different roles but all members have equal dignity and each member has a contribution to make and an opportunity to make it.' He went on to describe priests and bishops as midwives 'facilitating the birth of a different kind of church'.

The embarrassing truth for the Irish Church is that nearly forty years after the Second Vatican Council no 'birth of a new church' has taken place and, in view of all that has happened, or rather not happened, in the meantime, a safe prediction is that if we're waiting for priests and bishops to birth a new church, it simply won't happen. To paraphrase the Book of Revelation, if the baby is ever born can its future be trusted to the midwives of the clerical Church? (Revelation 12:4). On past evidence, demonstrably not.

We've been down that road and up that hill and round that mulberry bush huffing and puffing too often for words, even wise words, to mean anything anymore. For example, with the national pastoral audit I mentioned earlier, the word was that this time the bishops meant business. This, it seemed, wasn't the usual public relations guff. But the clerical cynics nodded their heads in mock belief because they knew from past experience that despite all the hype surrounding yet another initiative, the courage, imagination and leadership needed to slay the dragon of clerical control would once again not be forthcoming. Would the bishops be prepared to say that whatever the job is in the Church, that it should be entrusted to the person, clerical or lay, male or female who has the ability to do it? No. Would we be prepared to accept that those who are not ready to change must not be allowed to dictate the pace of change? No. Would we be we ready to move sideways or retire those who would once again try to stimey progress? No. Would we even be prepared to take out that clerical mind set and hold it up to the light of the day? No.

Unless the clerical caste system is dismantled, a people's church will never emerge. The priest on the pedestal is no longer, thankfully, part of the reality of Irish life but the extraordinary thing is that we have as a caste successfully inoculated ourselves against the realities around us. We behave as if preference is still some sort of a right, as if it's only a matter of time until (like latterday Napoleons on Elba, waiting for the call) our day will come again and these temporary difficulties will be behind us. As if lay people can be put in their place by using words like 'hierarchical' and 'ontological', as if dressing up in fancy clothes and awarding ourselves empty titles is anything more than a pathetic attempt to convince ourselves that we're more important than we really are.

How did all this happen? Where did this superior caste nonsense come from? It is instructive to look back into the past for the roots of a definitively clerical mind-set. Canon E. J. Mahoney's *Priests' Problems* was first published over forty years ago and it presents an insight into the clerical mind that is at once precise, remarkable and (with the benefit of the hindsight of the last twenty years) completely bonkers. For instance, 'in conscience the obligation of wearing clerical dress is a grave one, that is to say its non-observance is a mortal sin.'; 'unless a priest has an indult for celebrating (Mass) at sea, he cannot lawfully celebrate in an aeroplane'; 'the kind of reason which justifies the use of a woman server (at a convent Mass) is something less than grave necessity'; 'some commentators hold that the parish priest may not delegate his faculties for blessing vestments.'

How could anyone have believed all that casuistic nonsense? How could sane, intelligent and often holy men have bought such drivel?

That kind of 'advice' was being offered by way of what was described as, 'a valuable and popular feature in The Clergy Review,' during the 1940s and 1950s. Indeed so much to the point was it that it was edited by some judicious or injudicious canon lawyer and rushed into print as late as 1958! Is it any wonder that we are having such difficulty discerning the movement of the Spirit in our personal lives, warped as we have been for so long with so much rubbish? Is it any wonder that the clerical caste system we are immersed in is taking so long to break down?

No wonder indeed that the socialising influences to which we have been submitted in what passed for 'priestly formation' have had such a devastating influence upon us. Lessons learned not wisely but too well. And now we are left to cope with a clericalism that refuses to do the decent thing, lie down and die. The great beast is alive and well and still devouring everything positive in sight: imagination, initiative, creativity.

Clericalism pretends that the oil of ordination has created a distance from the ordinary and the normal and raised the ordained to a different and higher plain. Trent laid it all out for us in the catechism:

Priests are the representatives on earth of God himself. It is clear that their function is such, that none greater can be conceived; wherefore they are justly called not only angels, but also gods, holding as they do amongst us the power of consecrating and offering the body of the Lord, and of remitting sins, which has been conferred on them, transcends human reason and intelligence, still less can there be found on earth anything like it.

And Lacordaire summed it up in the great legend that adorned so many ordination cards of the past:

To live in the midst of the world with no desire for its pleasures; to be a member of each family, yet belonging to none; to share all sufferings, to penetrate all secrets, to heal all wounds; to go daily from men to God to offer him their homage and petitions; to return from God to men to bring them His pardon and His hope; to have a heart of iron for chastity, and a heart of bronze for charity; to teach, instruct, pardon and console; to bless and be blest forever; O God, what a life, and 'tis thine, O Priest of Jesus Christ.

No wonder we're the way we are.

Membership of the clerical caste was created by an uncritical acceptance of the dangerous theology and spirituality of the above extracts; it was confirmed by a belief that the 'ontological' change wrought by the laying on of hands conferred a right to a certain deference; it led to a presupposition that preference is our natural state, an acceptance that ordination presumes a power and an influence in religious matters quite at odds with personal ability, competence or intelligence; and it produced a separateness underlined by the wearing of the blackest of black suits. And even though the theology and spirituality that underpinned that clerical club has lost its place in the scheme of things, even though a privileged elitism is out of sync with the present age, even though we know that, confirmed in our sense of superiority and dressed in our clerical uniforms, we are like bedraggled refugees from another age, the fiction continues.

Part of it is that the Church is at a distance from the compulsions and the ethos of our time. Participation, responsibility, gift . . . the very language of the theology of baptism that resonates with the ethos of our day is distinctly at odds with a priesthood infected with clericalism. The siege that the modern world has laid at our door is being deflected by such august considerations as who might get the next parish and whether Fr Jack will be made a Monsignor and whether the sort of Monsignor he's made is red, black or lavender.

Someone told me a story recently about a man who always finished off the work of the day by closing the henhouse door. No matter how busy he was, no matter what distracted him, he just couldn't go to bed without pulling shut the rickety door of the henhouse. Or, as he put it, 'closing on the hens.' It became part of the ritual of his life. At that precise point in Irish rural life when the eggs in the fridge began to replace the eggs in the henhouse, a decision was made to let the hens die out. When his last feathered friend expired, the family wondered how he was going to retire for the night without the practiced ritual. They shouldn't have wondered. Hen or no hen, the same ritual continued. Every night for as long as God gave him breath, he persisted in closing on the non-existent hens. The ritual had become part of himself.

You'd imagine that it could hardly be clearer that

closing on the hens was no longer necessary and a short discussion would free people from a senseless activity. The problem though is that the obvious is not always recognisable from the inside. The perception of things from within the caste can be very different. If you are part of a tradition, it is very difficult to become part of the dismantling of the same tradition. If you give a wedge of your life to any activity, it is extremely difficult to stand back and set that work in realistic context. The bigger the institution, the more sacred the tradition, the more difficult it is to ask hard questions about it.

What happens is that an approach, a way of doing things becomes a tradition which in turns solidifies into a ritual. The ritual becomes part of a mind-set, a way of looking at life and at the world that responds in a knee-jerk way to every question, every possibility that life raises. And anyone who points out that the last hen has died speaks a language that those stuck in this mindset simply cannot understand. Or don't want to hear.

That enclosed, self-contained world bred a mindset and a series of rituals that became sacrosanct. Women covering their heads in Church, celebrants half-way through Mass getting into a dither because they began to wonder whether they were wearing the right colour vestments, communicants wondering whether it was fifty-nine and a half minutes since they had their breakfast or would it be the required hour if they waited at the end of the Communion queue, adults running in and out of the church in an effort to pile up indulgences - customs and practices that seemed central to the compulsions of life and that now in retrospect seem bixarre and nonsensical.

In a world where moral problems no longer seem easy to fathom, where the dilemmas of life offer no clear solution, where the carefully worked out wisdom of the past often seems bizarre in its simplicity, in that kind of world it is difficult to venture out of the cosy, self-contained world of the clerical culture that has infected our church and the mindset that comes with it. We need to name, as a matter of great urgency, the difficult truth that the hens are long since dead and gone!

CHAPTER SIX

The divine conspiracy

We are in a strange time. I have not a shadow of a misgiving that the Catholic Church and its doctrine are directly from God - but then I know well that there is in particular quarters a narrowness which is not of God. And I believe great changes before now have taken place in the direction of the Church's course, and that new aspects of her aboriginal doctrines have suddenly come forth, and all this coincidentally with changes in the world's history, such as are now in progress; so that I should never shut up, when new views are set before me, though I might not take them as a whole.

John Henry Newman

AMID all the prophecies of doom and gloom for our church, there is a sense in which these dark and difficult days may in retrospect be seen as a spring-time for the Catholic Church. Even the beginning of a new age. That may seem an optimistic opinion, in view of the circumstances - vocations in decline, practice in free-fall, leadership in disarray, credibility in tatters, priesthood in crisis. But the crisis for the Church precisely because the priesthood is in trouble may contain within it the seeds of creative change. Out of the ashes of a burned down forest shoots of new growth may produce a very different Church.

For one thing, people are finding their own voice. In Boston, Cardinal Law was told to resign by his own lay committees. A lay group calling itself *Voice of the Faithful* with the motto *Keep the Faith, Change the Church* has moved into the vacuum created by the failure of church leadership and the ineffectiveness of official church structures and, despite some official church opposition, has garnered an impressive level of support and legitimacy in the American Roman Catholic Church. Closer to home, lay structures are being re-examined by the clerical Church not because there's any great enthusiasm for a people's Church but because, with priests dwindling in number and in competence, there's no other choice. It almost seems as if there's a divine conspiracy to break the power of the clerical Church. Now that all the hints God gave us in the Second Vatican Council have been systematically ignored, could it be that what we see in these dark times is the rumour of God beginning to take a more pro-active role in the Church?

Let's look at possibilities arising from this divine conspiracy. First to come under the divine hammer could be the lack of accountability and transparency that was the fifth mark (after One, Holy, Catholic and Apostolic) of the Catholic Church. Decisions were handed down from above. No one knew who made them or why they were made and certainly no one ever expected to have to account for them. One of God's unlikely allies here is the secular State as the Tribunal of Enquiry, instituted by the Oireachtas, begins sorting out Ferns Diocese and later starts making its way through other Irish dioceses. A few timely enquiries into possible infringements of the criminal law has focussed the mind on the limits of canon law and produced a new-found respect for an ethos of transparency and accountability, an unexpected fruit of the nightmare of clerical sex abuse and the cover-ups that attended it. A transparent ethos could mean less of a focus on central control and more on local democracy. This will mean that people in parishes and dioceses will begin asking pertinent questions about finances. What money is collected? Who counts it? Who decides what it's spent on? How much money is in the account? Why are accounts not published in detail? Why has a priest the freedom to use parish funds almost at his own discretion? Once a few significant cases of financial mismanagement hit the tabloids, another train careering out of control will come down the tracks.

Another train *is* coming down the track. So far we have studiously ignored it when we could easily slow it down by introducing the kind of transparency into diocesan and parish financial accountability which is the right of the people and important for the protection of bishops and priests. It's even specified in the Code of Canon Law. (Though as we all know, such requirements are easily manipulated by the clerical system. A bishop once read out to his priests the requirement from the Code that members of the lay faithful should, with the bishop, form a diocesan financial committee. He then appointed the Vicar General, an archdeacon and a dean, three elderly clerics. After all, he said, they were baptised and therefore 'members of the faithful'. The message was clear: no lay person would be allowed to get their hands on the figures, no lay person would be allowed within the inner chamber). Of course a policy of openness could have particular repercussions for the heretofore secretive processes that attended appointments of bishops and priests.

Second, the decline of vocations could force a re-appraisal of seminary formation and a re-invention of a very different form of priesthood. Maynooth is now Ireland's only seminary with just fifty-five students. And D. Vincent Twomey, a lecturer in Maynooth, wrote recently in his book *The End of Irish Catholicism?* that 'three years ago not even one seminarian from the entire western seaboard, once a source of innumerable vocations, entered the seminary.'

Third, the scarcity of priests could mean the end of clerical power as we knew it in the Church. Canon law could delete the codicil that described Parish Councils as 'advisory' and a full-time lay parish worker could be employed to facilitate their organisation. Parish Councils could take control of parishes, organise fund-raising and in effect employ priests to be priests, not chief executives - to work as pastors, to say Masses and to lead liturgies organised by Parish Liturgy Groups and facilitated by lay liturgical experts. Diocesan Pastoral Councils could take over the day-to-day running of dioceses with lay personnel employed and their performance assessed. Ongoing diocesan synods could be part of the necessary structure of a People's Church.

Fourth, theology could become a more participative discipline with lay people making their rightful contribution, offering advice on areas in which they have direct experience. A more creative and compassionate response to issues like divorce and remarriage could be encouraged as theology becomes less focussed on law and more grounded in the pastoral experience of God's people.

The divine conspiracy could ensure the decline of clerical control, the oppressiveness that attended clericalism in all its forms and a sense of freedom and life for its adherents. It could create a space for God's People, 'ordinary' Catholics, to find their authority and to guide their Church with a surer sense of what is reasonable, truthful and possible. A lively self-critical Church would listen to people like the late playwright, John B. Keane, who remained a devout Catholic all his life but who was prepared to name unpalatable truths about the oppressiveness of the institutional Church.

This divine conspiracy taking the above form -

enforced accountability, decline of vocations, the growth of lay structures, the end of the oppressiveness of clericalism, the sweep of democracy - may be wishful thinking to some extent. Yet there is a case to be made for the belief that we are on the cusp of a revolution in terms of Church.

For a number of reasons. Few doubt now, after the Church's abysmal failure to deal with the sexual abuse scandals, that if lay structures had been put in place since the Council, lay people would instinctively have recognised that, in terms of dealing with such a complex issue, that the focus should be on the victims, the protection of children and full disclosure. The clerical leadership of our Church had to be dragged to that point as crisis followed crisis. Lay people would have instinctively focussed on the victim rather than, like clergy, instinctively defending the club.

Priests as a group are older, less competent, less energetic, more dispirited, battle-wearied and shell-shocked by the bruising the church has endured in recent years. It may be helpful to indicate a number of recognisable types.

Father Willing-but-not-Able comes in two versions. The older version is loyal to the end, prepared still to do his bit despite age having lessened his effectiveness. Most PPs over 60 fall into this category. They are, in the main, men of intelligence and ability but are caught in the deadly grip of clerical culture. They understand how critical things are. They can read the signs of the times. They can see what needs to be done. But the lessening of energy that age and a lifetime of hard work brings renders them ineffective in dealing with present needs.

The younger *Father Willing-but-not-Able* was ordained because they were gaps to be filled in parishes or because they were so long in seminaries that no one had the heart to tell them the truth - that for everyone's sake, including their own, they should leave or be asked to go because they were neither able nor suitable for the task in hand. The hope was that they might survive in a rural parish somewhere but after ordination the problems appeared. They lack judgement, can't cope with the cut and thrust of life, have little energy, are prone to illness and often have have to be 'covered for' by older clergy.

Father Able-but-not-Willing is usually in his '40s or 50s. He is intelligent, competent, able. But he's thrown in the towel in many respects and he feels dispirited and bored. He's in need of renewal but can't find the energy to take a sabbatical to recharge his batteries. If he's a PP he will do the minimum in his own parish and pace himself towards retirement. If he's not a PP he will keep his head down so that he'll get a parish and once he has his own place he'll pace himself towards retirement. *Father Able-but-not-Willing* can be arrogant - feeling diminished by ineffective leadership, diocesan mismanagement, the ordination of embarrassingly unsuitable men and the general decline in the status of priests. If he was younger and had other possibilities he'd opt for the unreason and inconvenience of the lay life. When he has a drop of drink taken he'll concede that he regrets not having packed his bags years ago.

Father Weary has been around the parish track a number of times. He's tired of the incessant grind of parish life. After 35 Holy Week ceremonies, 502 marriages, 647 funerals and 830 baptisms he has decided that he can no longer function at the level he used to. He's impatient with former interests (once he had a thriving liturgy group and produced impressive plays); he's distrustful of energy (once he built a parish hall); he's sceptical of the value of the work he has done and the contribution he has made; and he's rattled by the emergence of what he perceives as an over-demanding and super-critical laity. So he feels he's been there, done that if not worn the tee-shirt and others would say he's burnt out. His twin ambitions are to be appointed to a small undemanding parish and survive as a priest because he's too old and too tired to contemplate a different existence.

Father Disillusioned was once full of idealism and possibly a bit naive about the way things operated in the Church. He's a holy man and he's made the mistake of imagining that everyone has the same interest, enthusiasm and standards as himself. He's appalled and a bit scandalised by the level of cynicism among the clergy and the political manoeuverings for position among the careerists. But what has confirmed his disillusionment is the appointment of incompetent people to very prestigious and demanding positions or careful men who lack the very qualities of imagination or creativity the particular positions demand. Like all those caught in the slipstream of such appointments he is dispirited by the fall-out from such promotions and the unwillingness of any group - diocesan or deanery conferences, Council of Priests - to surface the issue. He would never solicit a particular position for himself - he would regard it as improper and inappropriate to do so - but he now knows that it is common practice. He often wonders if the clerical culture around him is a form of cancer to Christian living.

Father Do-little sits at the back of every clerical meeting, pouring scorn on the proceedings. It is part of a sub-conscious process of ensuring, in so far as is humanly possible, that nothing will disturb the ease and tranquillity of his measured existence in this world. Do-little can't abide committees of any description and has a ferocious antipathy to Parish Pastoral Councils. He dislikes meetings, scorns whatever paperwork arrives from diocesan office, which he professes never to open. He plays bridge and golf and watches the American Golf Tour and the European Golf Tour every Thursday through Sunday on *Sky Sport* which enters his life through that most sacred of clerical artifacts, the satellite dish. While most of his golfing buddies feel guilty about letting their golf interfere with their parish duties Dolittle would never let his parish duties interfere with his golf. An outside observer might describe him as lazy or in love with his own comfort but this would be to underestimate the energy he puts into doing nothing even when he has little enough to do. He is fond of saying that his ideal parish would be one where there is no parish hall, no parish liturgy group, no Parish Pastoral Council, no parish church and, preferably, no parishioners.

Father Pious lives in a world of his own. He is on pilgrimage most of the time, to Lourdes, Fatima, San Giovanni and Medjugorje. He was ordained on a tide of piety and, against all the odds, the tide hasn't gone out yet. He has a very strong devotion to Our Lady and has one of Padre Pio's gloves. Elderly ladies love mothering him. He in turn delights in their affirmation and is the recipient of legions of pairs of black socks and an orchard of apple tarts. Of benign disposition, he doesn't understand much of what's happening around him and would be mesmerised if someone asked him about his level of morale. While the church may be falling down around him, he's selling tickets for a raffle for an extension to the church in Medjugorje and distributing pictures of Our Lord of Divine Mercy.

Father Ennui is usually in his middle years and finds in his life a progressive listlessness or ennui, a difficulty motivating himself, a peculiar restlessness and unease that he can't quite shake off. He has begun to reflect a bit about how abnormal his life is and how things seem to be closing in around him. Sometimes he panics a bit about his future when he realises how isolated and unwanted older priests can be. He finds the prospect of retirement at 75 frustratingly distant and wonders if it's possible for anyone to give 50 years of service to anything.

Father Ready-Willing-and-Able is a man of interest, enthusiasm and weight. There aren't too many like him around anymore. But he's ready, willing and able to move with the times. He wants to acknowledge the problem, analyse the situation, agree on a strategy and get on with it. He feels disrespected when he finds out that decisions are already made but the consultation hasn't taken place yet. He's aware of how out of sync the Church is with the contemporary world and is impatient with those who find it easier to condemn the world rather than engage positively with it. *Father Ready-Willing-and-Able* is probably in his late 30s or 40s or early 50s. He believes in consensus, competence and character and the abolition of the seniority system. He probably isn't a PP yet and probably has a PP whom he's either minding or tolerating and who is exasperating everyone in sight.

Of that gallery of seven clerical types, only one has any real sense of the kind of church we need if the gospel of Jesus Christ is to stand its ground in Ireland in this new century. Most priests are part of the problem rather than part of the solution. The conclusion, clear and uncontestable for me, is that priests (even if it were appropriate that they should) will not drive a new church. We are not up to the job. The fact that we are dwindling in number and ability may be God's way of forcing that truth upon us. The divine conspiracy.

CHAPTER SEVEN

Priesthood at the heart of darkness

In the small hours of the night, when the voices murmur inside me and there is no one to call, I wonder was I too careful, too trusting, too loyal, too good for my own good. Should I have staked more of a claim to my own life, even if it flew in the face of accepting God's will? Should I have chosen a warmer life? Would it have been better not to have fallen into a life I sense now I may never have wanted? Would it have been better, all things considered, to have let my life be, to have kept more of my life for myself, to have claimed a greater human freedom?

A Pastor's Diary

THERE is, we're continually told, a perceptible decline in morale among priests. Writers now regularly seek to define a certain dispiritness in our ranks, a bit more perhaps than the clerical equivalent of Scott Fitzgerald's 'thinning briefcase of enthusiasm'. The writer Micheál Harding catches, with disconcerting accuracy, that vague emptiness in his image of the priest sitting in his armchair, 'staring at the telly and thinking that it is a terrible world'. Even Edward Hoagland, a non-

Catholic, writing in Harper's Magazine has captured
something of that ennui or disenchantment:

> *I tend to gaze quite closely at the faces of*
> *priests I meet on the street to see if a lifetime*
> *of love has marked them noticeably. Real*
> *serenity or asceticism I no longer expect,*
> *and I take for granted the beefy calm that*
> *goes with Catholic celibacy, but I am*
> *watching for the marks of love and often see*
> *mere resignation or tenacity.*

Possibly, some of us might add, with good reason. For
one thing such disenchantment is more than understandable: the paedophile scandals; the failures of church
leadership; vocations in free-fall; the haemorrhaging of
significant sections of our congregations; the perception
of an anti-Church media bias; and, not least, the feeling
that we have become endless and usually disparaging
news. In the worst of times, mere disenchantment is
understandable but there is, I believe, somewhere beyond
disenchantment, a darkness in priesthood that we need to
explore, shadows that we need to hold up to the light.
Micheál Harding explored this hidden ground in his
bleak and disturbing work *Priest* and more recently I
heard a psychotherapist tell an audience of priests that
there was something around sexuality and priests that we
needed to explore. There's something awry at the core of
priesthood and it is surfacing now that priests, bereft of
the traditional support-systems, are more isolated and at
risk.

I think we need to describe that dismal place, to
acknowledge some difficult truths about the Irish
priesthood, to hold the lived reality of priesthood up to
the light of the day, to own the shadows. I think we need
to address the possibility and the pain as the foundations
shudder around us, to name that terrible sense of isolation

and loneliness that Bishop Brendan Comisky alluded to on his return from America, after undergoing treatment for alcoholism. We need to explore that place where isolation births a palpable and debilitating emptiness, where the wonder disappears when normality reasserts itself, where the landscape between distraction and difficulty is completely bare and you begin to wonder whether this is what God intended.

> *You may have acquaintances, few friends:*
> *Besides your unreplying God you have no*
> * confidant.*
> *Nevertheless you lift your hat to all. Old*
> * ladies*
> *Especially will seek you out, sometimes a*
> * sinner*
> *You are guest at many celebrations, a must at*
> * birth or death.*
> *Sometimes you wonder whether this is how*
> * God intended it.*
> *(Padraig J. Daly)*

I want to mull over that place. I want to inspect that piece of ground and see whether there is space in it for a life, a human life. I want to ask questions about whether, when we take off the black suit of duty, when we divest ourselves of function, there is anything left for ourselves. Once a priest, always a priest. But is that enough? Or is there anything more? I want to pause in that place because I sometimes detect a terrible desert of the human spirit behind the experience of priesthood today. I detect an appalling price being paid in isolation and loneliness and it seems quite often that no one is paying much attention.

I sense that isolation in the restlessness of the spirit that seeks out the ordinary and the normal. I watch it in the extraordinary construction of a comfortable but

unfulfilling life support system, often no more than a
bizarre hobby that makes do for a life. I measure it in the
perceptible increase in nervous disorders. I sense it in the
half remark, the knowing shake of the head that often
paints a brittle and a bitter clerical landscape. I have
come to resent the timid, circumspect involvement of
those who know what's happening but find a safety-valve
for their own feelings in the pious clichés of another age.
*Say your prayers, lads. Recreate among priests. Look
after God and God will look after you.*

First, what that isolation is not. This desert without a
spirituality is not some form of Promethean discontent,
the sort of existential pessimism that inevitably
characterises the mid-life years. Nor the unbearable
heaviness of being that some modern philosophers are
wont to speak of. Nor the coping with the demons of
failure and regret that pickle every human life. Nor is it
the contemporary perceptible and predictable decline in
morale and the dispiritedness it inevitably engenders.
Nor the kind of deterioration that takes place after a
lifetime of dull routine invades our souls and corrodes
our spirits. Nor indeed the contemporary malaise known
as *Burn-out*.

Rather is it a growing unease that the kind of
normality of life that eases us into old age is simply not
possible within the parameters of our present existence. A
quiet voice, like a delicate flute, complaining in the
distance, disturbs our small hours reminding us that the
normalities which help humanise our lives - personal
freedom, independence, intimacy - have passed us by.

> *Supper over, can you picture him there*
> *Slumped in his chair by the red fire*
> *Listening to the clock's sound, shy as a mouse,*
> *Pattering to and fro in the still house?*
> *The fire voice jars; there is no tune to the song*
> *Of the thin wind at the door, and his nearest*

neighbour
Being three fields' breadth away, it more often seems
That bed is the shortest path to the friendlier
   morrow.
(R.S. Thomas, *The Minister*)

What is at issue here is not a 'normal' experience of a sense of isolation usually exacerbated by the passing of the years and may perhaps be a necessary condition of celibacy, or indeed of life. Nor the social isolation that a sense of aloneness necessarily exacerbates. Rather the very context of our lives seems to render an abnormal degree of isolation almost inevitable. There is, I believe, in the lives of many priests a debilitating isolation that makes human contact an ambiguous experience. Factors that help to produce that isolation include our own unrealistic expectations of ourselves, the shifting parameters of respect and disfavour we now enjoy and endure, the increasing demands of an educated and articulate people, the progressive decline in morale due to the media mauling we periodically experience and the failure to address its implications.

For one thing the contours of our existence are rooted in the oppressiveness of clericalism. That presents as the oppression of others but, with clericalism, the greater recipient of oppression is, in effect, the priest himself. Quite apart from the separateness and isolation that shaped the quite bizarre seminary formation most of us received, we ingested a dismissive clericalist mentality to the non-ordained that viewed position and power in terms of ordination rather than ability. Unease with the concept of the priesthood of the laity, in effect the rights of the baptised, found us laying down the law as a protective moat against the encroaching world. And there followed almost imperceptibly a drifting into the clericalist mould: a presumption of preference; an assumption of power; and a membership of a clerical caste.

Clericalism, like other systems, can be comfortable and convenient. Meals spontaneously appear, queues suddenly divide like the Red Sea, Father (even when he knows very little about anything) is often told that he invariably knows best about everything. A retinue of elderly ladies acts as a life-support system: darning socks, knitting black cardigans and tut-tutting about priests in neighbouring parishes with less traditional wardrobes.

There is of course a price to be paid: the words we use, the sensitivities we respect, the way we dress, the smallness of the world that rule and convention allow us to inhabit. But accepting the boundaries, playing the role, inevitably predicates an oppressiveness of which the priest is often the ultimate victim. Ordinary people have a way of playing the system, paying lip-service to the parameters, feigning support for its wisdom but ultimately placing it all in the context of an eccentric clerical world that, like the Trinity, they couldn't really be expected to understand. They have enough to do making ends meet, watching Coronation Street and worrying about their teenagers. Meanwhile, the priest is at home reading his breviary, putting on his Roman collar before he answers the door and organising the annual outing for the Pioneers: playing the role until a small insistent voice begins to ask him where his life has gone. *Sometimes you wonder whether this is how God intended it.*

Some recognise the definitive oppressiveness of the clerical system and claim the freedom to break free. They have the courage to live semi-independent lives, wearing ordinary clothes, developing mature and committed friendships, refusing to play the appointments games of snakes and ladders, giving a wide berth to the exclusively clerical dinner circuits that narrow the vision, cramp the spirit, limit the space and that ultimately contrive to snuff out any last vestige of independence or normality - in effect claiming a freedom to live, within the limitations of place and time and priesthood, an ordinary life.

But they are the few. The many simply fold under the system, at once enjoying its rewards but ultimately sensing how destructive it is of them as people. The more they recognise how oppressive the clerical world is, the more they realise they lack the courage to extricate themselves from it. And the more they become aware of that world breaking up under their feet, the more paradoxically they feel the need to hang on to the remnants of it. Like long-term patients who can't function outside an institution, limiting though it be, so many cannot envisage a different world or a different life. They find themselves clinging to the wreckage of a disintegrating clerical culture. Young men who left the seminary now dazzle in the more demanding worlds of commerce and academia while some of their more gifted colleagues who were ordained find themselves running bingo for the GAA in a parish hall. John Hegarty, a seminarian for the diocese of Tuam, was a classmate of mine in Maynooth. He left the seminary after four years, did a Ph.D. in Galway, further research in the University of Wisconsin and worked for Bell Laboratories before being appointed professor of laser physics in Trinity College. Now he's Provost of Trinity. If he had been ordained for Tuam, where would he be now, PP of Aughagower or, if my grandniece Martha will one day forgive the implied diminution, a curate in Killawalla? And John O'Donohue - poet, philosopher, writer, gifted speaker and best-selling author of *Anam Cara* and *Divine Beauty* - was, after returning from post-graduate studies in Germany with a Ph.D., appointed to a curacy. It would have meant giving up his writing; he couldn't reach an accommodation with his bishop; and he left the priesthood.

The field of dreams that opened out before us on ordination day is now for many a thicket we try to break through to preserve the vestiges of an *ordinary* life. In the small hours and the quiet moments, questions surface about the wisdom of the whole enterprise and our role in it. What is left of me when so much is subsumed into priesthood? What can I do now to live a human life in the time God gives me? We find ourselves living at an angle to the ordinary world, but we can no longer justify our institutionalised patronising of the ordinary. We may march to the beat of a different drum; we may try in our own fashion to witness to a truth beyond the obvious; but we end up wondering why the ordinary and the normal are by definition beyond the comforts of the ordained, why the fusion of the everyday and the holy merits so little attention. Is God not found in the ordinary and the everyday? If so why do we insist on what is different if not abnormal when the loss is so palpable and all the evidence is that the reality is so problematic?

As the sands of time trickle inexorably away, we become aware of the oppressiveness of the clerical caste, of the dehumanising effect of that oppression and in some instances of the pathetic existence that passes for a life. 'Is this it?' we ask. If we take away the function that is represented by the black suit and the Roman collar, what else is left?   Consider this extract from the anonymous author of the *Intercom* column, The Pastor's Diary (2002):

> *I could see her tripping over a half-made sand-castle, losing interest in its construction and someone calling from a distance, Be Careful, Don't go out too far, Don't do that! And then I realised it was my voice calling, scolding, encouraging. Her name was Caroline and once I said her name to myself I realised she was one of the daughters I never had. And then she ran towards me, her eyes squinting up into the sun, and she was laughing, laughing,*

laughing at something someone said and I could feel my heart heave with happiness.
I woke crying, trying to remember the dream, wondering what it meant. Was it, as I reach the end of my life, a half-cry for an ordinary life, a grieving for the children I never had? Or just a scene from a film that flickered across my consciousness and that melted into the air - my mind playing tricks on me. Or a kind of re-alignment of the forces within me being brought into some kind of normal synthesis - Nature having a last laugh at my unnatural state.
Sometimes I find myself standing at a street corner and, for a fleeting moment, imagining that the young man coming towards me is my son or a young woman, the mother of my grandchildren. I want them to stop and acknowledge my existence. I want them to warm my life. I want to be wanted, even as a peripheral presence in their lives. Invariably they just smile at me wondering whether they might know me from somewhere and move on, leaving me feeling foolish. An old man wistfully seeking to lay claim to a life I never had.

This experience of long-term isolation and the loneliness it engenders could well be the key to understanding much of the shadow side of priesthood in Ireland today. Why do so many of us become so aggressive and so arrogant about position and status? Why is there such a sense of emptiness and futility in the lives of so many priests now? Is this not why parents, who sense that something is awry, actively discourage their sons from choosing priesthood? Is this not why so many priests are ambivalent about encouraging vocations, reluctant even to preach about them? Even, asking whether there may be some connection between inappropriate sexual attitudes and actions and a desperate, inarticulate cry from a lonely heart for some vestige of warmth and comforting.

These are difficult questions and they revolve around the unease and the sense of disconnectedness and dislocation associated with the experience of priesthood today. It is not that priesthood should be restructured so as to dovetail with the compulsions of our time. But rather that for priesthood to be lived there is a balance to be achieved between the need to witness to values beyond the world and the need to live a normal life. There is an equilibrium to be sought that pays its dues both to priestly and personal integrity, a working correlation that promises a mutual enrichment rather than demands the terror of isolation.

An image from Seamus Heaney helps to make the point. A basic theme of his collection, *The Spirit Level*, is the need for balance and equilibrium. The poem *Weighing In* highlights the poet's consideration of the subtle reciprocal economies that make our lives workable and bearable. The poem starts with the image of a *56lb weight. A solid iron / Unit of negation.* It is *squared off and harmless-looking / Until you try to lift it, then a socket-ripping, / Life-belittling force.* But balance this unbearable weight against another "On a well-adjusted, freshly-greased weighbridge" and it becomes manageable. Suddenly, almost imperceptibly we find ourselves in the arena of ethics, psychology and religion which Heaney comments on harshly,

Passive
Suffering makes the world go round.
Peace on earth, men of good will, all that
Holds good only as long as the balance holds.

As long as the balance holds. My contention is that the balance in priesthood between function and person, that would enable a more enriched and effective priesthood and a more normal personal life, is no longer there. No one wants to name the obvious yet difficult truth that unless the priesthood is restructured to facilitate the living of a more normal life then the *problems* will continue to increase. The difficult question we don't want to face is: why are parents looking at the lives of priests and praying that their sons won't join us?

That and other questions need to be addressed. Until they are we have to ask whether it is fair to encourage young men into priesthood without a support system that will help them cope with an experience of long-term isolation and loneliness that may break them? And until they are we won't understand why so many priests are now looking back the long tunnel of withdrawal from human kind and wondering whether, in the years left, they need to opt for a more human existence, a more normal life. And until they are we will see more priests in their fifties and sixties just walking away from priesthood in a last desperate search for a less oppressive, more ordinary life. And until they are we will see too many priests sinking into depression in isolated presbyteries until eccentricity becomes oddness and oddness becomes the inability to function at a human level, even to the extent of making breakfast or taking a shower or dusting the dandruff from our shoulders. And until they are, priests will struggle on to breaking point, some believing they have no claim on the warmth and affection that is the right of every human person; others no longer buying the sublimation theories - *priests are different, offer it up, sure, everyone has problems* - that aged leaders work out at a safe distance from members of the human race; and still others, God help us, slowly waiting for it all to end so that the pain will be over. And more and more we wonder whether this is how God intended it.

Deep down we know that this is not how God intended it. We know that we have to distinguish between the essence of priesthood and the cumulative accretions of history, between what *is* and what can be, between the *what* and the *why* of the Church's law. And we know too that sooner rather than later we will have to develop alternative structures if the priesthood *as a life* is to stand its ground in the modern world. The seriously dwindling numbers entering seminaries is further evidence of the problem. Footsteps can speak louder than words and, in emptying corridors, they reverberate. So we have to bear the burden of change and to challenge the mind-set that can't imagine a priesthood apart from the institutional accretions that keep the deeper questions at bay and that refuse to acknowledge the darkness at the heart of it.

We have to find new ways of being priest in a changing world. To do that we have to recapture that spirit of enquiry, that openness of mind, that widening of horizons, that sense of life and energy that the Second Vatican Council ushered in where we felt empowered by a communal search for the fullness of God's truth. We have to listen to what the Spirit is saying to the Church. New wine, new wineskins. Museum or garden? Change or decay?

CHAPTER EIGHT

The care of priests?

And what is the upshot of this lack of heat, this lack of heart? The upshot is that he is sitting alone on a Sunday afternoon in an upstairs room in a house in the depths of the Berkshire countryside, with crows cawing in the fields and a grey mist hanging overhead, playing chess with himself, growing old, waiting for evening to fall . . .

J. M. Coetzee

FOR the last few years an elderly priest has written an anonymous column in *Intercom*, the in-house Irish bishops' magazine for priests. Under the title *A Pastor's Diary*, quoted in the last chapter, he writes in instalments a convincing and realistic portrait of a rural parish. In reflective mood he presents some of the foibles and eccentricities of his parishioners, his own oblique slant on his life and work and, most tellingly of all, the gradual disintegration of his own life as he becomes increasingly aware that the sands of time are running out. Some have protested that the picture he paints is too bleak, that the portrait lacks any human warmth, even that he's suffering from depression and needs help! My sense of his writing is that all of that misses the point. He writes, quite obviously, from within. Much of what he says resonates with many priests as the letters column regularly testifies. There is a bleakness there surely but isn't there a bleakness about the end of life anyway, especially a priest's life when much of what we do can't be quantified, when we have lived and probably will die on our own, when the Church is in such difficulty and when we find intimations of our own mortality around every corner?

Not that that's the whole story. But it is part of it and what makes this writer's thoughts interesting, even compulsive, is that he's not into denial, he doesn't try to write straight with crooked lines. He pays us the compliment of his discomfiting honesty. For example:

> *Priesthood has had a deadening effect on me, at one level making me more than I am and at another somehow making me less than I might be. Marriage and children for all their unease and inconvenience connect to life, link into a vein of vitality and energy that is beyond me, outside my life. I seem one-dimensional, predictable, dispassionate. Sometimes on a summer's evening as the sound of children's voices carry on the still air and the ghost of loss gets into me, I mourn for something other that I might have been, for a different life I might have lived . . There is a weight I carry - tradition, circumstance, conviction - that deadens on my shoulders and that frays a part of me that seeks comfort and warmth. It is a strange*

feeling. It is as if, in these emotionally egalitarian times, that part of me has to stay its hand, that I am above or beyond or outside the normal and the ordinary. And I sometimes wonder what that has done to me, what corrosion of spirit has taken place, what iron has entered my soul . . .

I recognise the provenance of these moments. A priest friend who has retired has discovered that after a lifetime of priesting there is nothing of himself left when he subtracts what he does from who he is. It is as if the sum of his life was the function he performed and the deficit was camouflaged by a suit of black clothes.

As the years slip away I sense a similar diminishment. It is as if I am living between places, between worlds, a kind of ruptured identity. The priest in me has stymied the person I might have become. And as I come to the end of my life I sense the sharpness of that loss.

In the first part of my life, when the blood was warm and everything seemed possible, what I was seemed less than what I might be and everything was charged with possibility. And now that I have less time left what I was then seems so much more than what I am now and everything is marked with ending, closure, death.

This is more, I feel, than the universal regret and individual guilt that pickles every life: promises unkept, potential unrealised, songs unsung, the diminishing returns of an odd and unquantifiable life. And not just a cri de coeur lamenting the bleakness of the emotional landscape of my life. But rather a growing sense of a loss beyond words because I didn't trust the hungers of the heart and the dance of the soul.

I was, I think, all things considered, a reasonably good priest. So I took, as the Americans would say, the road less travelled. I trusted in God's providence. Accepting my lot; deferring to others; obeying my PP and bishop; distrusting the quest for fulfilment and identity as selfish and individual; distancing myself from friendship and intimacy; seeking perfection; and, I have to say now, in the process at a human level, effectively diminishing myself . . .

Would it have been better not to have fallen into a life I sense now I may never have wanted? Would it have been better, all things considered, to have let my life be, to have kept more of my life for myself, to have claimed a greater human freedom? I resonate with John O'Donohue's words: I would love to live / Like a river flows / Carried by the surprise / Of its own unfolding.

But I didn't. So I wake at night and a great wave of loneliness sweeps over me. In the dark small hours I sense the contracting of my world and the ending of my life. If I got a heart attack now, who would I call? If I couldn't get to the phone, when would I be missed? Sometime tomorrow possibly or maybe even some day next week? And no one close enough to give me courage when the owl calls my name. No housekeeper even to hear my call in the night, to sense my sense of the end of my life. Is this what it means to grow old?

I give that extended quotation because I believe it should be compulsory reading for those involved with the care of priests. It points up how limited the lives of priests can be at a human level, how isolated both physically and psychologically so many priests are, how difficult it is to deal with the closing in of your life when you are *a man apart*, how much in need of support priests can be.

There are bachelor types in priesthood who love the single life, who want to live on their own, who bask contentedly in their celibacy, who can't understand why anyone would be unhappy with the solitariness and un-ordinariness of a priest's life and they will say that the above quotation is self-indulgent gibberish.

But there are others, many others who will read that quotation and worry about what will happen to them when their health begins to deteriorate and their world contracts. They will look back on their lives and wonder why so little was said or done about actually helping them to live a celibate life, to cope with the struggles and inconveniences of parish, to prepare for retirement. They were launched into priesthood and left to survive on their own. They sense that no one really cares about them or what becomes of them. They sense that there's no structure that can or will deliver the level of support and care that they need to live out their days with a modicum of dignity and self-respect. They feel the Church dying around them and in a very different Ireland they feel taken for granted or patronised or even regarded as figures of fun. Once they were on pedestals; then they were shuffled off them, now they don't really matter, apart from the occasional functional or honorary role on the sidelines.

There's an eerie silence or vacuum that many priests are waiting for someone to fill while at the same time sensing that no one quite knows who or what might fill it. Work goes on; the daily grind of pastoral care brings its own momentum; respect is earned at a personal level; but there is evidence of a paralysing unease and unhappiness among priests as they try to work out what has happened to their world.

There is anger among priests too. Anger that the leadership of the Church is ineffective, incompetent and even sometimes non-existent. Some bishops seem to be living in a different world. Terrible mistakes have been made and there seems to be almost a constitutional inability to admit the mistakes, to accept responsibility for them and to learn from the experience. And that failure of leadership is percolating down into parish life, distressing priests, undermining their confidence, diminishing their status, damaging their relationship with their people.

Many priests stood at their pulpits the weekend after the desolate and damaging *RTÉ Primetime* programme, *Cardinal Secrets*, and wondered what their people were saying about them. Many hadn't the confidence or the skill to address their people's fears or their own sense of betrayal and they ended up saying nothing. Exacerbating their sense of unease and desolation was the inability of people to support them or to understand how isolated and discomfited they were. When priests die or move to other parishes the ritual tributes can be fulsome but returning to their empty presbyteries that weekend was, for many, a lonely and haunting experience. Some received a few phone-calls of support; for others, the sound of silence felt distinctly ominous.

For more, it underpinned their sense of being regarded as useful functionaries at parish level but without any real sense of community or family support when the going gets rough. Some felt that the anger of people was being directed (unfairly) at the most accessible representative of the Church, the local priest. Who will speak out for priests? Bishops no longer have a credible voice in that regard. If priests speak themselves it will be dismissed as self-serving. And, reaping the whirlwind of our failure as a church to give our people their rightful place, there are no lay people in positions of significance to confront unfair comment or to defend or support the individual priest working at parish level.

I spoke recently to a PP who had worked for more than 40 years in his diocese. He wanted to retire, not because he felt he had nothing to contribute, but because he felt discouraged and disillusioned by the leadership of his Church and by the lack of support from his people.

All the work that priests and religious had put into education, all the salaries pumped back into schools, all the extra curricular activities to give children from deprived backgrounds an opportunity to be educated, all the investment in boarding schools for the children of the rich and the middle-classes - and they just took it and walked away, without any sense of the mountain of work put into it or even a suggestion that a word of gratitude might be appropriate.

All the efforts at parish level to build churches, to resource schools, to develop community, to support the elderly, to encourage the young, all the meetings over all the years, all the counselling of people in distress, all the hidden support of people in abject need – and at the end of the day, he felt, who cares? People just take it all for granted and priests and religious are left feeling empty and dejected. We've heard the negative stories of abuse and no one would say that they shouldn't be told. Of course they should. But where are the other stories? The 99 others, where are they? And the question - who cares for our priests? – who wants to be part of the answer?

There's a feeling of reserve, suspicion, even of distrust among priests about the present national crusade to 'care for priests'. Is there a legal imperative involved in case someone goes berserk and a bishop or diocese, by way of defence, can point to some expensive process of care that was in place to circumvent such an outcome? Is the celibacy issue, which is at the heart of the care issue, not being addressed because an unacceptable level of resentment and anger might surface? Can a diocese really care for its priests in any satisfactory way, especially if the care is confined to a carefully chosen committee of clerics? Are priests being spun a public relations exercise that has no substance behind it and ultimately will leave those depending on it even more disillusioned?

There's a simple test which tells whether a diocese is serious about caring for its priests: look at the priest in the diocese who is in most need of care and examine the record. And if that priest happens to be someone who has betrayed the trust of his people and diocese by sexually abusing children then the record speaks for itself. In a prophetic article in *The Furrow* (April 2003) Fr Eamonn Conway, a priest of the diocese of Tuam and Head of the Department of Theology in the University of Limerick, raised the question about what happened to priests who had abused, served prison sentences, may have left the formal priesthood through their own decision (or under duress) and now find they have nowhere to live, no one to turn to, no place to belong. His conclusion was that the Church has to acknowledge a duty of care to these men.

It's not an easy thing to say, because caring for sexual offenders will win few marks for anyone in the current climate. As well as that it may seem like the Church 'looking after its own' and under-appreciating the damage these men have done to the innocent. Conway's article is certainly not guilty of any of that and he argues the case trenchantly.

Caring for offenders, he says, is part of the ongoing protection of children. Sexual offenders, laicised and turned away from their dioceses, may be a continuing risk to children and if they abuse again how convincing will be the case a diocese offers that the individual concerned was laicised and that therefore the diocese was no longer responsible for him – especially if the individual testifies in court that he was laicised under duress? Is there not some form of obligation that past offenders, especially those said by the courts to be a continuing danger to children, be monitored and given ongoing therapeutic treatment? Are victims not entitled to every assurance that their abusers will not offend again? Another consideration is that the Catholic Church, even if only for the pragmatic purpose of avoiding further litigation, has to insure that if a clergy offender re-offends, that structures were in place to protect children.

I get the sense that in future years priest sexual offenders who were bounced out of priesthood and whose dioceses didn't accept obvious responsibilities of monitoring them and supplying therapy for them will once again be embroiled in litigation. The neglect involved will be interpreted as a washing of our hands of continuing responsibility and another example of the kind of institutional denial that has marked the Church's response over the last decade and beyond. Dioceses which disown their priest offenders may regret that questionable strategy in time.

There's a more important consideration. We are continually being told that the Church is a family. Every diocese is a family. And if a member of that family gets into trouble we stand by them. It's not that we accept their wrongdoing in any way. We reject the sin but we don't reject the sinner. We expect that of ourselves. More importantly Jesus Christ expects that of his followers and his Church.

Isn't there something shocking about a priest who has gone to prison, accepted laicisation not because he wanted it but because it was suggested strongly to him (possibly even by his bishop) that there was no alternative, served his sentence, come out of prison, has nowhere to go, no place to stay, no one who wants to have anything to do with him, no money and a diocese (his former family in faith) who would prefer if he got lost somewhere. So he goes from place to place trying to eke out an existence, struggling to find a flat, looking for work, afraid to draw the dole in case people learn he has served a sentence for child sexual abuse and run him out of town.

The Catholic Church in Ireland has had to learn some hard lessons in this difficult and complex area. Surely another lesson we have to learn is that for everyone's sake we have a responsibility to care for priest offenders. It mightn't be a popular thing to say but someone needs to say it.

The Irish Catholic Church has been on a steep learning curve for some time. First accepting the reality of child sexual abuse offenders within the clergy. Then understanding that offenders couldn't be 'cured' by some psychiatrist. Then realising how the situation was exacerbated by moving offenders around. Then appreciating, to some degree at least, something of the pain and damage inflicted on the innocent. Then accepting that wondering what our founder, Jesus Christ, would do about the whole sorry mess was more important than getting advice from lawyers. Then introducing a process for dealing with accusations. Then accepting that in significant cases we ignored our own process. Until eventually accepting that the Catholic Church had to admit responsibility and negligence.

I deal at some length with this challenge to the Church - caring for priest sexual offenders - because the reality of the official neglect and spurning of these men has shocked other priests. When we ask ourselves, in the small hours of the night, what's the worst thing that might happen to us, we see an ascending litany of ills from heart-attacks to strokes to disabling car accidents to false accusations of sexually abusing children. And the questions we're left with are: Who would stand by me? who would support me? Who would *care* for me? If those most in need of support, solidarity and care are in effect eased out of or forced out of priesthood and diocese as embarrassments to be sidelined, what kind of priority will I be if something happens to me? The terrible truth is that priests no longer trust their bishops or their dioceses to provide an acceptable level of care because bishops seem more interested in covering their backs and dioceses more interested in limiting responsibility. Official Church policy sometimes seems to emanate more from legal chambers than out of a gospel imperative.

This distrust of bishops and what is perceived as an uncaring Church is eating away at the confidence and self-assurance of priests. Many are trying to make lives for themselves while struggling to survive within priesthood and church. Others are organising secular incomes of varying descriptions and buying houses because they are fearful of what might happen to them in later years. Still others are just walking away from priesthood. Like Fr Oliver McTernan, a PP in Notting Hill in West London for over twenty years and a regular contributor to BBC Radio Four's *Thought for the Day*. His faith, he says, is as strong as ever but he is frightened to stay on in active ministry because, as he told *The Tablet*, he has seen so many of his friends, 'turn almost into eccentrics because they kept trying to carry on in isolation.'

We learn slowly, very slowly, as a Church. We act only under pressure. We move very cautiously. Can the Irish Catholic Church learn to care for our priests while we still have them?

CHAPTER NINE

Celibacy: the strangled impulse

In his extreme youth Stoner had thought of love as an absolute state of being to which, if one were lucky, one might find access; in his maturity he had decided it was the heaven of a false religion, toward which one ought to gaze with an amused disbelief, a gently familiar contempt, and an embarrassed nostalgia. Now in his middle age he began to know that it was neither a state of grace nor an illusion; he saw it as a human act of becoming, a condition that was invented and modified moment by moment and day by day, by the will and the intelligence and the heart.

John Williams

THIRTY-FIVE years ago, Karl Rahner in 'The Celibacy of the Secular Priest Today: An Open Letter', (in *Servants of the Lord*) dealt with 'the burden, the riddle and the challenge' of human sexuality as experienced by celibate secular priests. Even though he endorsed celibacy as an appropriate life witness for secular priests, Rahner's essay remained remarkable, *á la* Johnson's dog, not so much for what it said but for the fact that it addressed the subject at all. The theology of marriage and its clearer implications emanating from the documents of Vatican II had placed large question-marks over the traditionally superior status of the celibate vocation. Around that time, Charles Davis, albeit for doctrinal reasons, had very publicly walked away from both priesthood and celibacy. And a steady trickle from the active priesthood sounded a clear warning for a still buoyant conciliar church. The celibacy factor, though not discussed at the council, seemed about to take centre stage. There were even suggestions that priestly celibacy would go the way of Friday abstinence!

Now, years later and with the benefit of hindsight, we look back with wry amusement on Rahner's careful words. You'd imagine that in a more open, confessional world, the celibacy issue and related questions of intimacy in a priest's life would be more widely discussed. But that's not the case. There's no real debate about celibacy - even though at least one hundred thousand priests have left the ministry, vocations in the first world are in free-fall, more and more priests believe that celibacy should be optional, overwork and stress are progressively becoming a feature of a numerically declining and fraught priesthood and the percentage of homosexual priests and seminarians is significantly higher than in society at large. Hard questions are being asked about the relationship between compulsory celibacy and the pathological side of priesthood that has emerged in recent years and yet can you remember anyone of note writing anything of significance about celibacy in the last three decades?

There is, I believe, a need to open up the celibacy question, to air something of the pain and the promise of that charism, to question some of the easy assumptions, not to say presumptions, of those who want to parrot the official line and insist on bending experience and theology to fit the received wisdom, to enrich the experience of a freely accepted celibate commitment, to face the reality that enforced celibacy is no longer a credible or defensible discipline at a personal, ministerial or theological level.

There are intervals in history during which the nature of knowledge shifts definitively. It is no secret that in the area of sexuality a decisive shift has affected the world and consequently the Church in our lifetime. A deeper understanding of sexuality leading to a new sense of what human nature is has questioned the intellectual framework of Catholicism. As far back as the late 1970s, the novelist David Lodge fictionalised that shift to telling effect in the accurately observed and hilarious novel, *How Far Can You Go*? And we recognise that shift when a panelist on *The Late Late Show* recently excoriated the Church for visiting what he called 'buckets of Catholic guilt' on innocent teenagers by insisting that bad (that is, sexual) thoughts were mortal sins. 'Sure,' he said, reasonably enough, 'if we hadn't bad thoughts wouldn't there be something wrong with us!' We see the shift in thinking in the wide-eyed belief that nowadays greets erstwhile stories of priests refusing to sit in a car with a woman in deference to an old canonical requirement. Or of presbyteries in the past that had separate staircases for housekeepers. Or solicitous nuns encouraging their teenage charges not to indulge in close dancing, 'to leave room for the Holy Spirit to get through'. Or Bishop Tom Ryan ringing *The Late Late Show* some years ago to adjudicate on proper honeymoon attire when he would have been better taking his Bovril early and going to bed. It was all so outrageous and so recent.

Now it all looks narrow, obsessive, unbelievable, obsolete. Yet a few decades ago it was taken with deadly seriousness as part of the Catholic worldview. Indeed it still is, in some places. A few years ago at a retreat in Rome a Cardinal from some Vatican congregation told an international gathering of priests that they had no need to love another person, it was sufficient to love the Church!

The revolution in our understanding of sexuality is the backdrop against which the link between celibacy and priesthood needs to be viewed.

There is no doubting the value and the witness of a voluntarily assumed celibate commitment. Since the time of Christ it has been an accepted and valued pattern of Christian discipleship. Jesus was a celibate and the so called 'eunuch' text (Matthew 19:12) would seem to indicate the importance of celibacy chosen for evangelical reasons. Another consideration is that celibacy witnesses to the next world as a counter-sign of the permissive ethic of our age and it can free people to minister to those on the margins of society thereby confirming its witness value in a world given to assessing everything in material terms. It is also argued that celibacy can make a priest more available to his people, afford him more time for prayer and make priesthood more cost-effective. It has been directly linked with priesthood since the fourth century and necessary for ordination since the thirteenth century. And in the new Code of Canon Law its connection with priesthood has been reaffirmed once again.

As against all of that there's no indication in the Scriptures that presidents of the eucharistic assembly should not marry. Indeed Timothy 3:2-5 indicates the opposite - the presumption was that most of them should be married. The development of the Church law of priestly celibacy is not, as we know, unconnected with the gnostic notion of sexuality as a pollutant and notions of ritual purity. Other considerations are as follows:

- because of the decline in vocations faith communities are being unnecessarily deprived of the Eucharist, with priestless parishes now becoming a reality;
- fewer people are nowadays prepared to commit themselves to lifelong celibacy so the celibacy requirement encouraging vocations to the Catholic

priesthood is becoming progressively more difficult to sustain and there's a constant steam of resignations from priesthood, often associated with celibacy;

- the development of a theology of marriage and the recognition that sexual abstinence in itself does not constitute holiness or virtue has tempered the significance of a celibate way of life;

- the universality of the celibacy law is blurring the very charism it is meant to foster;

- in some cultures the non-acceptance of a celibate way of life diminishes its witness-value;

- there is growing evidence that priesthood exclusively linked to celibacy attracts an unhealthy percentage of homosexual candidates;

- in the wake of the clerical child sexual abuse scandals, the focus on the sexual lives of priests is placing significant question-marks around celibacy and how it's being lived;

- at a time of heightened sexual awareness and changing sexual mores, there is the twin difficulty of communicating what the witness-value of celibacy is and actually living it;

- and, for those who resent the fact that they didn't choose celibacy directly, that they had to accept it as part of the package that goes with priesthood, there is the diminution of living what for them is an abnormal life without the warmth and solace of an intimate sexual relationship and the enhancement of priesthood that attends it.

It is difficult to avoid the stark conclusion that the universal celibacy requirement for priests is damaging the charism of a freely chosen celibate commitment, limiting the ministry of priesthood, facilitating accusations of using priesthood to disguise sexual orientation, encouraging suggestions of problematic sexual behaviour and condemning normal men to living abnormal lives when they feel called to priesthood but not to celibacy. It seems incredible - in view of the evidence before us and since in theological terms the Church has always accepted that celibacy is not a prerequisite of priesthood - that, rather than accepting the logic of our time and the rhythm of our age, elements in the Church are fighting a rearguard action, desperately trying to drum up support for continuing the present Church law and even suggesting (in the face of tradition and theology) that celibacy is of the essence of priesthood. While the growing consensus among many theologians and church-people is that the debate is over and that compulsory celibacy is no longer conducive to effective ministry and that it is only a matter of time until the celibacy requirement for priesthood is readjusted, there's a certain irony about the fact that the only writing now about celibacy is from a small coterie of people, out of tune with the needs of our church and the spirit of our age, who believe that defending the status quo is the optimum response.

One part of that approach is to sideline all the arguments against compulsory celibacy by dismissing as 'disloyal' those who challenge the official position. Another technique is obfuscation. Witness a contribution from my classmate Bishop John McAreavey in *The Formation Journey of the Priest : Exploring Pastores Dabo Vobis* (Ed. McGregor/Norris, p.99) which dismissively rejected in a few sentences a series of positions in favour of *optional* celibacy by arguing for the *value* of celibacy, as distinct from its necessary association with priesthood.

Another is the presumption that the reason why the official position on celibacy is not accepted is not that the point has been rejected but that the whole matter has not been adequately explained. This is what psychologists call 'the Education-Enlightenment hypothesis', the theory that convinces us that by telling people what makes sense to us, it will eventually make sense to them. Supply the right information, give the proper instructions and people become so enlightened that they accept what you say. An example of this is Thomas McGovern's *Priestly Celibacy Today*. McGovern, an *Opus Dei* priest, writes that Pope John Paul is, 'conscious that often it (celibacy) is badly explained, and has gone so far as to say that the widespread view that celibacy is imposed by law "is the result of a misunderstanding".'

McGovern attempts to put things right by responding to the Pope's desire, expressed in *Pastores Dabo Vobis*, to see celibacy presented and explained more fully from a biblical, theological and spiritual perspective. The difficulty is that while the exercise is laudable and legitimate it presents as a defence of priestly celibacy but ignores the important distinction between the *value* of celibacy and the limitations of *compulsory* celibacy. As well as that the usual bogeymen are blamed for the present confusion. Different philosophical and theological attitudes, he says – some of which have been 'borrowed from Protestantism' – have surfaced over the past thirty years and have served to muddy the traditional concept of priestly ministry. Then there are those modern cousins – relativism, scientism, utilitarianism, individualism, democratisation and the privatisation of morality. Added to that are the social and cultural pressures of the present time and (inevitably!) efforts to undermine celibacy in sections of the media and even among some sections of the clergy themselves.

McGovern's thesis is this : the primary and essential explanation and function of celibacy is its ontological participation in Christ's own priesthood and his spousal love for his Church. To give this claim substance he trawls the scriptures and the history of the Church. Even though he accepts that there there are no scriptural texts which directly link celibacy with the ministers of the Church, 'the scriptural validation of priestly celibacy

derives more from the convergence of meaning of a
number of different texts, and the cumulative thrust of
their significance, rather than the probative value of
individual texts'. This, with respect, won't do. It is a form
of spin-doctoring, using scripture to advance a
predetermined thesis. It has no credibility.

Similarly with history. 'The memory of the early
Church,' he writes, 'and the testimony of the Fathers is
that the Apostles, whatever their marital situation after
being called by Christ, lived perfect continence
thereafter.' How does he know? And what sources does
he use to support this thesis?

Until recently the general historical perception was
that the Church didn't articulate a law of celibacy until
the fourth century. This view was established by one
Franz Xavier Funk, the ecclesiastical historian, in the last
century. But, McGovern argues, Funk based his
assessment on a document now known to be spurious. It
seems that the intervention of an Egyptian monk-bishop,
who gloried in the name Paphnutius, who supposedly
intervened at the Council of Nicea in 325 to reject any
plan to impose the discipline of absolute continence on
married clerics, is not all that it seems. What's more,
Funk made a basic error in identifying the concepts of *ius*
and *lex.*

The reality is that we know so little about the first four
centuries, and that applies to Roman history as much as
Church history, that we can't really be sure of very much
apart from general outlines. Reading back into history
has no credibility. The fact is that a scripture scholar or a
historian could take McGovern's sources and other
sources as well and advance a cogent argument for
conclusions diametrically opposed to the conclusions of
his book.

Another soft target is the media. In a preface to *For
Love Alone - Reflections on Priestly Celibacy,* Cardinal
José Sanchez rejects the perception that celibacy is

responsible for declining numbers and blames the media for the current unease. The gist of his argument is that there is a slow but steady rise in ordinations worldwide and this should take care of what Adrian Hastings once called 'a real eucharistic famine' spreading from Africa, Latin America and even reaching the United States and Europe.

There is an alternative wisdom, a different perspective, a more long-term loyalty to the present teaching on priestly celibacy. Long and complicated dissertations on the scriptural, historical and theological development of the law of celibacy that attempt to establish a necessary link between celibacy and priesthood are unhelpful and, perhaps, dishonest. There isn't any such link. And we know that there isn't and all the footnotes in the world won't convince anyone that there is.

Celibacy is not intrinsic to priesthood. There have been married priests for more than half of the present history of the Church. There are now married Roman Catholic priests (former Anglicans) and, despite the decretals of Pope Siricius in the fourth century, nobody is suggesting that as ministers of the altar they should be 'perpetually continent'. Few people doubt now but that in the future (as in the past and as in the present) there will be both married and unmarried priests in the Roman Catholic Church. Already in parishes in England married Catholic priests, formerly Anglican, are replacing Catholic priests who have left the priesthood to get married! The weight of history and common sense is moving the Church away from Funk's Folly and the decretals of Siricius. What we need is not a refusal to deal with the real world but a theology that can stand its ground.

We need, too, a calm and honest debate. To argue for a change in the celibacy requirement for priesthood is not to argue against celibacy. The value of the charism of celibacy in the Roman Catholic Church is not at issue. But a celibacy freely chosen would enrich the Roman Catholic priesthood and enhance the witness of celibate priests. What we need in this debate is not a one-sided trawl through patristics and a list of quotations from a series of worthy documents but a large dose of reality and a full measure of common sense. An acceptance too that money and power are part of the politics of this debate.

A few years ago, when a gallant effort was being made to defend the ministry of altar servers from the clutches of small female persons intent on scaling another male bastion, a draft document from a canon lawyer justifying the prohibition of altar girls was doing the rounds. Should it be promulgated officially, people wondered? The consensus was 'to leave things be' and how wise it was. At this time of writing it seems that the Church has survived the introduction of altar girls.

When the rule linking celibacy to priesthood is eventually amended, as no doubt it will be, many of the defensive tracts that now seek, even demand, our attention will be seen to owe more to an undiscriminating enthusiasm and short-term loyalty than the long-term good of the Church. Some causes are defended not wisely but too well.

CHAPTER TEN

Authority in decline

If all you have is a hammer, sooner or later everything looks like a nail.

John L. Allen

Those who have been intoxicated with power can never willingly abandon it.

Edmund Burke

IN his recent book *The Courage To Be Catholic*, George Weigel, the celebrated biographer of Pope John Paul II, argues that the crisis afflicting the Catholic Church has to do not with sex or authority but faith and 'fidelity'. In the quarter century following the second Vatican Council, he says, many Catholics, including many priests have held back from committed belief in 'the full teaching' of the Church and have thereby fallen out of 'full communion with the Church'. The reason for this is 'the culture of dissent' that has emerged in the Church since Vatican II and Weigel traces this 'culture of dissent' to a specific incident, what he calls 'the Truce of 1968'.

After Pope Paul VI issued his encyclical, *Humanae Vitae*, nineteen priests in Washington D.C. publicly repudiated it. Cardinal Patrick O'Boyle disciplined them. In 1971 the Vatican's Congregation of the Clergy issued a document minimising the nature of the dissent and 'urgently' recommended that Cardinal O'Boyle should remove the sanctions imposed on the Washington Nineteen. Under duress, Cardinal O'Boyle agreed. It was understood that Paul VI wanted 'the Washington Case settled without a public retraction from the dissidents'.

This, for Weigel, was where Aughrim was lost. Paul VI, nervous that insisting on a retraction would lead to a schism, was willing 'to tolerate dissent on an issue on which he had made a solemn, authoritative statement'. The effect of this failure or mis-judgement was to encourage disagreement and 'a culture of dissent' was born. 'The net result of this remarkable incident,' Weigel writes, 'was to promote intellectual, moral and disciplinary disorder in the Catholic Church in the United States.'

For Weigel, the sequence is clear. The Washington Nineteen led to the culture of dissent which in turn led to indiscipline and to a questioning of authoritative positions and to an effective declaration of being 'out of communion with the Church'. This led to the priest killing his conscience 'on matters relating to his own behaviour, including his sexual behaviour'. And this in turn led to the crisis of child sexual abuse which in turn was compounded by the failures of episcopal leadership. Q.E.D.

It is, I'm afraid, too simple because, like those who trace the death of traditional authority in Britain to twenty past seven on the 1st July 1916 - the first day of the Somme, when sixty thousand British soldiers were slaughtered due in large measure to the negligence and incompetence of their superior officers - it is too neat to say that if only Paul VI had taken a different line with the Washington Nineteen the subsequent history of the Catholic Church in the United States would have been different. The fact is that dissent from *Humanae Vitae* wasn't confined to nineteen people in Washington but extended through a large swath of the worldwide episcopacy.

The more complex truth is that traditional authority was dying in Britain long before the Somme. The more complex truth is that traditional Catholicism was dying too, long before the Second Vatican Council or *Humanae Vitae*, because the world was changing, people were changing, wisdom was becoming less amenable to pre-packaged dogma. An authority of rank was giving way to an authority of competence. Authority was becoming something you earned. It's no one's fault. It's just the way the world is and we have to face it rather than imagine that we can undo it. Isn't that what the Second Vatican Council was about? Engaging with a changing world? Old truths in new wineskins?

A late and revered parish priest of mine, Ben McLoughlin, loved to hold forth on the Sunday meanderings of his early priesthood in the parish of Kilcommon, near Belmullet in Co. Mayo - territorially, the largest parish in Ireland. It was the early Thirties. He was at one end of the parish and his fellow curate at another. His PP at the time, of unfond memory, insisted that the curates conduct Rosary and Benediction in each other's churches every Sunday evening. This involved, for both of them, a round trip by bicycle of about thirty miles on dirt roads. Every Sunday evening their paths crossed twice, on the journey there and back where they discussed their respective Rosaries and Benedictions and, no doubt occasionally at least, their PP. It was a distressingly authoritarian league that insisted everyone play away games every Sunday.

Some years later, in the same parish, when a priest's house was being built, the curate involved had his application for an inside toilet rejected on the anatomically curious but socially respectable grounds that it wasn't a PP's house.

Forty years later, again in the same parish, a PP and his curate had a heated argument over a particular pastoral strategy. The PP shot his last remaining barrel when he suggested that his opinion should prevail because, he said, 'I'm the PP'. The instant 'So what?' rejoinder of his cheeky curate indicated that, in the interpretation and exercise of authority, certain rumblings were being detected. If not quite the Somme, at least in Kilcommon a certain leakage.

In more recent times, it could be argued that a comparable diminution in authority took place. There is no need to labour the details. The theology of episcopal authority is unchanged, the outward appearances are stoically preserved but a whole series of bridges have been washed away. A reverberation of Richter proportions has shaken the foundations of trust and acceptance and a lethal mist of antagonism and silence has spread across the land. Rank still claims a certain respect, but a respect that is often put on hold until the individual earns the authority that heretofore was simply an adjunct of the office.

Authority is becoming more and more ethereal. Politics, big business, the legal system, the Royal family in England and not least the Church have failed very public examinations in the last few years. There is a perception of disconnectedness on the part of traditional authority figures from the compulsions of life as it is lived next door. Princes are tape-recorded without their knowledge and their utterances, somewhere on the continuum between embarrassment and tedium, headlined in national papers. Priests are regularly lectured at about 'ordinary' life as if they never left their presbyteries or heard confessions. Bishops often seem to have less authority than Eamon Dunphy or Bart Simpson.

In an increasingly complex world, the power of authority ultimately depends on consent. What people now respond to is an *authoritative* authority, not an *authoritarian* authority. Consensus is the ethos of the day; participation, the compulsion; and those who deny that logic do the Church little service.

In Church terms, there is a distinct aura of retreat, a steady refusal to contemplate the changing nature of authority and its implications for the Catholic Church. The covered wagons have been moved into a circle and what welcome there is seems reserved for those who play safe games and make quiet noises in the secluded interior. Those who reinforce prejudices about the big bad world out there get more of an audience than those who feel that the Church has to live in it. There is no truck with the real issues of the day: couples living together; the question-mark that Catholic marital practice has placed over traditional birth-control teaching; the identification of religion with morality; the ignoring, even the cynical hectoring, of papal, synodal and episcopal injunctions to laicise the Church; the sense of disconnectedness between what comes from the sanctuary and what is experienced in the pew. Indeed there often seems a distinct reluctance to disturb the mythical status quo. The emperor is always fully clothed. A paralysing prudence has been substituted for a pressing analysis. Already the future seems to be behind us.

Loyalty may, for some, be a consoling sweet to suck on but it transposes itself into a none-too-subtle form of fundamental disloyalty when it is used to conveniently sidestep the very issues that the Church needs to face. Loyalty, or what passes for loyalty, has of course too the added bonus of apparently claiming the higher moral ground. But unquestioning loyalty is, in effect, a contradiction in terms. The question remains as to how

best the Church is served: by those who massage the egos
of decision-makers or those who are prepared to disrupt
the futile equilibrium of an institution at odds with the
real world. One honest voice calling out an unpalatable
truth may serve the Church a thousand times better than
the silent many who simply do what they are told in a
spirit of uncritical loyalty.

We need to give terms like 'loyalty' and 'authority'
contemporary meanings that will celebrate the modern
climate of consensus and participation and the prevailing
winds of intelligence and reason. We need to accept that
the traditional understanding of authority invested in a
few individuals who attain a certain rank is out of tune
with the rhythm of our age. We need to forge a very
different kind of authority if we want to converse with the
world we live in. Because unless we do, then authority,
through scepticism and that distancing that ends up in
ironic relief, will be undermined or even eroded beyond
repair.

There is now, in society and in Church, a pervasive
decline in what Archbishop John Quinn in an Oxford
Lecture called 'the model of control'. Yet we refuse, at an
institutional level, to recognise that fact. While the world
speaks a language of accountability, transparency and
openness, we are defensively sponsoring a more
traditional creed.

For some, this embracing of a defunct and discredited
approach is an ideological stance, a final but despairing
effort to keep out the tide of the modern world. Yet even
in the most rural of parishes, the demands are the same:
for democratisation not oligarchy; for partnership not
tyranny; for community decision not individual edict; for
participation, not domination; for accountability not
secrecy; for, in Archbishop Quinn's words, 'a model of
spiritual discernment not a model of control.' Because
whatever about the larger issues, the struggle for the
future of the Church will be won or lost at local level. The

parish, or in rural parts, the church area, is the coalface of the Church. And the unpalatable truth is that in general the present clerical leadership of the Irish Church seems to lack the confidence or the competence to respond to the modern agenda. The mystique of the black suit is no longer a sufficient refuge against the demands of the world.

We need a more broadly-based and reflective authority emanating from a wider and deeper consultation among the People of God, lay and clerical, and drawing on the expertise, experience and wisdom of lay people who will of necessity have to be deployed in leadership capacities in dioceses and in parishes. In clerical terms, this may seem a consummation devoutly to be avoided but I think we're sufficiently in touch with our own deficiencies to recognise the inevitability of some new form of structured lay leadership in our parishes.

This suggestion isn't something pulled out of thin air. The historical evidence of lay people participating in decision-making processes in the Church, (as Ladislas Orsy shows in *America*, April 1996) from at least the fourth century to well into the twentieth century, is overwhelming. For instance, it seems very clear that Lady Abbesses exercised some quasi-episcopal jurisdiction over a specified area and the clergy serving in it. We need to reaffirm in some structured way the Vatican II insight on the priesthood of the baptised rather than the redefinition which sees power as deriving exclusively from ordination, a prescription which to my knowledge has no basis in law and which has spawned a diminished theology of the laity and a consequent diminishment of their role.

There is nothing in the law of the Church which prohibits lay people being involved in decision-making processes: voting as members of synods and councils, including Vatican Congregations; accepting responsibility for the financial affairs of parish, diocese or Church; even being appointed Cardinals, as I indicated earlier. The block is not in the law of the Church which, as we know, can be selectively quoted to prohibit any real degree of participation. The block is in the grip that the clergy have on the Church. The time has come to let faith, as Orsy puts it, seek not only understanding but practical action.

This direction is implicit in the recent formulation of a 'Pastoral Plan for Killaloe Diocese'. A working committee of lay people, religious, priests and bishop was set up in Killaloe in response to a call for a realistic and focussed plan to be drawn up following widespread consultation. What emerged was that while people still hold to spiritual and moral values and are especially open to contact with church at key moments in their lives there is 'some form of paralysis in the church' which has prevented a creative response. The antidote to this, the document says, is for committed lay people, men and women, to be included in the ministry of the church. The church must connect with the lives of the people, speak in their language, engage with their stories. The good news we bring is the unique worth of every person, the closeness of God to us, the building of relationships of love. These are in tune with the deepest longings of our hearts and the best intuitions of our culture.

The Killaloe Plan suggests that new structures will need to be set in place: at parish level (Parish Pastoral Councils); at cluster levels, to enhance co-operation between neighbouring parishes (Regional Pastoral Councils); and at diocesan level, to provide co-ordination and support in the delivery of pastoral priorities (Diocesan Pastoral Council).

We are approaching a decisive turning-point for the Church. Whether we can take the tide of change is another question. Old institutions and old habits die hard.

CHAPTER ELEVEN

New kinds of leader

*The Vatican commonly chooses as bishops men who are
at the far end of the conservative scale, despite the
tensions and alienation that such a factional policy
generates. It seems to regard courage, imagination and
creativity as dangers to be avoided in bishops, opting
instead for the type of leadership which finds safety in
doing nothing - like the bishop who announced in the
cathedral, on taking up his new appointment, 'I'm not
afraid to say no.'*

Owen O'Sullivan, OFM Cap.

A new kind of authority demands a new kind of
leadership, a new kind of appointments process. The
key words for the individuals involved and for the
process which appoints them are 'transparency' and
'openness' and with a focus on what the demands of the
particular responsibility will be. 'Co-responsibility' is the
word the Second Vatican Council had for it.

A new authority / leadership will mean an end to
promotions systems enveloped in secrecy and confined to

the clerical establishment and it will mean a wide-ranging and effective process of discernment within the Church. It will also mean an end to the appointment of 'safe men' who will forever plough the same furrow as their predecessors. They are exactly the kind of leaders the Church can no longer afford.

In the difficult times we live in, when collective nerves are often frayed, we can sometimes imagine, in our efforts to live in a very different world, that in Yeatsian terms everything is falling apart and that the centre cannot hold. The temptation is to place an emphasis on a policy of retrenchment, holding the line, reorganising the troops in defensive mode. In sailing terms, this is to ply the shallow waters along the coast, not to head out for open seas. The temptation is to avoid the very qualities we need – a spirit of adventure, imagination, creativity.

It is, in the times we live in, a limited, defeatist view. Promoting members of the second team to the A squad simply because they have a certain talent for defensive strategies may in the short-term seem to contain the situation but when captains need to be appointed and players need to move into combative positions, the limitations of a retinue of corner-backs become all too obvious.

While it would appear that a safety-first disposition, a controlled imagination and a reluctance to offer an opinion on anything of substance seem curious qualifications for leadership in a society where the storms of change are raging around us, the discomforting truth is that *The Safe Man* is once again enjoying his place in the sun. Who would have thought it?

I have long felt that what we needed most in the Irish Church was a plague on the house of *the Safe Man*, a pestilence on prudence. Never was that benign malady more sorely needed because *The Safe Man* is everywhere. And you can spot him a mile away. He may, under pressure, offer an opinion on whether it is raining or not but he will insist on not being quoted. Nobody will ever know what he thinks because he will not commit himself to an opinion on anything in case he may have to revise it tomorrow. And if he does make a comment, he will preface his words with 'As our Holy Father says in . . .' A favourite word to describe everything is 'interesting' because it neatly combines an impression of support without any quantifiable commitment. As a holy insurance against any kind of original thought, he repeats clichés in case he might inadvertently give something away if he used the wrong word or phrase. He says nothing. He begins nothing. He changes nothing. He tables no motions and is reluctant even to second anything - waiting as he does for every motion in life to be carried unanimously. The goal of *The Safe Man* is to give the impression of activity without in fact allowing anything to happen. And at the court of the unconventional, he will ensure there is never enough evidence to convict him.

Not that *The Safe Man* is a new phenomenon. Sixty years ago Fr Neil Kevin, professor of English in Maynooth College, described *The Safe Man* as 'of the race of men who invented the proverbs':

> *in the case against Safe Men, it is to be noted, that commonly we have owed more to those who took a chance and seemed to fail than to those who always played safe and seemed to succeed. On the ruins of the failure of yesterday the success of tomorrow is often built. The paradox of the man who is ahead of his time has a still finer point - the Safe Men save their age from him but he saves the succeeding age from the Safe Men.*

So what kind of leaders do we need? If a consultancy firm was asked to head-hunt suitable candidates as bishops in this new and very different Ireland, how would the personality profile shape? Possibly someone who is holy but not pious, creative but controlled, decisive but balanced, approachable but reserved, consensual but clear, agreeable but opinionated, humourous but not funny, media-friendly but stage-reserved, above all a leader who goes where he wants others to follow.

While it is true to say that such paragons probably exist only in the foothills of a pious imagination, a church-wide process of effective consultation has a better chance of surfacing such individuals than the present system. For instance, the present consultative process will hardly surface that kind of candidate. For three reasons. One, even the most loyal church activists seem to have lost confidence in it. Every few years a letter comes from the bishop's house asking for three names in the event of a vacancy in the diocese. When a vacancy arises, a list of three names or *terna*, as it is called, is sent to Rome and no one seems to know what happens between the arrival of the list in Rome and the announcement of an appointment. The Apostolic Nuncio has overall responsibility for the process; the bishops of the province have a say; the archbishops of Armagh and Dublin are probably consulted; and a few carefully chosen laypeople may be asked for their opinion. But the whole consultation is so cloaked in secrecy that accusations of individual and political influence are not easily answered.

Another difficulty is that Apostolic Nuncios can get tetchy if the process is tampered with in any way. In one diocese, after a prayerful and reflective few days of discernment were spent by the clergy, it was unanimously agreed that one name would be sent to the Apostolic Nuncio and the retiring bishop and the Council of Priests were asked to endorse the decision. Nothing was heard from the Apostolic Nuncio.

As a result another meeting of the priests agreed to

send a representative delegation to the Nuncio to confirm the original decision. The Nuncio received the group graciously but pointed out firmly that while he was always available to meet priests and discuss their concerns such delegations of priests were not part of the official process of the appointment of bishops. He suggested ominously that the priests of the diocese should consider the appointment of St Irenaeus who lived just after the time of the Apostles and, though not the choice of priests or people, was a great success as Bishop of Lyons. The implication, not lost on the delegation or on the priests to whom they reported back, was that the appointment of an outsider was imminent. (The delegation could have mentioned that St Ambrose, a layman who was made bishop of Milan by the public acclamation of the people, but that wouldn't have fitted the present political climate. The clear conclusion was that an Irenaeus, from a far country, rather than an Ambrose, one of their own by acclamation, was to be expected.) The delegation was told to return to their diocese and to inform the priests that they should welcome 'with joy' whatever bishop the Holy Father sent them.

At a subsequent meeting, despite the Nuncio's reservations, the priests confirmed their original decision to recommend one priest and that decision was communicated to the Nuncio.

In the event, the decision of the priests was completely ignored and a priest from the other end of the country was appointed bishop. While the priests made no secret of their unhappiness that their considered, reflective and prayerful process of discernment had been dismissed and their status in the whole process disrespected, the appointment was loyally accepted and the new bishop graciously welcomed and received. This mature handling of what was an awkward and delicate situation owed much to the generous welcome of the priests, the

sensitivity of the new bishop and very little to the process
of appointment which is clearly in need of reform.

A worrying feature of the present dispensation is that
those responsible for the process seem to have no
appreciation of how little faith priests have in the process
and how disrespected priests feel when legitimate and
respectful concerns are pushed aside. It seems only a
matter of time before an appointment will be rejected by
a diocese of angry and disrespected priests with all the
damage and embarrassment that will cause within a
diocese and for the Church. All it will take is a letter to
The Irish Times by a group of disaffected priests rejecting
an appointment and everyone will wonder how it has all
come to this.

A second reason why the present consultative process
will hardly surface the right kind of candidate is that the
laity are presumed not to have any opinion. It's said that
some 'members of the faithful' are consulted. Who they
are, who chooses them or who they represent no one
seems to know. It is, in effect, no more than a formal,
limited deference to the fact that the clergy are not the
only members of the Church which Vatican II defined as
'the People of God'. It is difficult not to argue that our
theology of church demands that laity be given a real say
in the appointment of bishops and difficult not to
conclude that the present exercise in ecclesiastical spin is
disrespectful and patronising.

A third reason why the present consultative process
will hardly surface the right kind of candidate is that the
clerical church is in effect replicating itself every time it
appoints a bishop. The Vatican authorities, it seems, have
a particular template: a priest in his fifties or sixties, who
is sound on *Human Vitae*, is very much in favour of the
traditional form of Confessions, never writes or says
anything that might be interpreted as critical (and when
he does write or say something he quotes the present
Pope every second sentence), has a lively Marian

devotion, gives priests' retreats and befriends the bishops of the province. Creativity, imagination, an ability to approach reality at an oblique angle, a prophetic disposition, in tune with the rhythms of our time, an independent mind - are not, to put it mildly, valued characteristics.

Inevitably too, bishops will search out someone in their own image, clerical clones that help them to convince themselves of their own suitability. Priests too - without a proper, prayerful and reflective discernment will be tempted to seek a popular, undemanding, non-confrontational figure who won't upset the tranquillity of their lives. Which is why the present *consultation*, if that isn't stretching the word too much, can be focussed in terms of 'getting our own man' in the expectation that you know what your getting.

Part of the difficulty is that there's a clerical type who imagines himself to be *episcopabile* (bishop material) and who spends his life preparing himself for the call from the Navan Road (Nuncio's address). He massages all the relevant egos, makes all the appropriate noises, goes on all the correct pilgrimages, visits all the right people, wears black socks and will always be seen to have the breviary under his arm or at least within easy reach. Loyalty to the institution is a core value to such an extent that if the Pope announced that there were six or even sixty-six persons in the Trinity instead of three he would have no difficulty incorporating it into his faith. He wouldn't admit to anything as secular or individualistic as ambition but is a dangerous leech on the church politic because he knows what needs to be said but he will never say it. Or at least not until the mantle has passed him by. His need to be a bishop should automatically exclude him because anyone who would want to be a bishop (including those who, over the course of a lifetime, assiduously prepare for it) are, for that very reason, definitively unsuited for it. There are of course

those who, in the manner of the smooth Bishop Devoy in
Father Ralph (by Gerald O'Donovan, Brandon Books
1993), desire:

> *a quiet - unfortunately it was never
> accomplished - country parish with time for
> meditation and prayer. God willed
> otherwise. Perhaps I said 'Nolo episcopari'
> too often and to punish me this burden was
> placed on me.*

Similarly, the appointment of priests needs to be
revamped. It is unacceptable that, like De Valera looking
into his own heart and deciding what was best for the
Irish people, a bishop would look into his heart and
decide what God wanted. Wouldn't an appropriate
discernment process be more fully of God if it came
through a sensitive consultation with the People of God,
aware of the needs of their own parish, and the
willingness and ability of prospective PPs or curates to
respond to such needs? This would be one way of getting
around the often insuperable obstacle represented by
some priests who imagine that they actually own the
parish, can abolish structures built up gradually and
carefully by their predecessors over many years and can
decide by way of personal edict what will or will not
happen in their parishes. It also solves the problem of
coping with impossible priests, some in secular terms
well past their sell-by date but in canonical terms still the
right side of the generous retirement age of 75.

It would also force younger priests to recognise,
accept and execute a basic job specification apart from
what they might like to shape for themselves. A difficult
truth in the Irish Catholic Church is that at a time when
the pews are becoming noticeably uncrowded, when the
demand for competency reverberates through Irish life,
many younger priests are quietly rejoicing in a new

respect for the old wisdom of control and domination and are scampering back to the cul-de-sacs of the past. While the world speaks a language of accountability, transparency and openness, they are defensively sponsoring a more traditional creed.

What priests need are support systems in their parishes that will free them to serve rather than to control, to be priests rather than chief executives, to be part of a team ministry of laity, clergy and religious rather than Lone Rangers riding their own private ranges.

How different the response to our present difficulties would be if we had engaged with the world, as Vatican II taught us to do, instead of circling the wagons. It is instructive that in a recent book on the crisis in the Catholic Church in America, *A People Adrift*, Peter Steinfels, the former religion editor of the New York Times and a shrewd observer of the interface between society and institutions, writes that the paedophilia scandal, rooted in the evil acts of individuals, became an institutional disaster because of 'a failure of leadership'.

So what can be done? It seems increasingly imperative to confront one of the last bastions of clerical privilege in the Church, the seniority system, which allocates responsibility on grounds of age rather than ability. Regardless of a much wider consultation, it seems that unless a bishop is prepared to set aside the seniority pecking-order when it comes to appointing priests and to accept short-term personal unpopularity for the long-term good of the Church, then clearly we will remain the agents of our own demise. That's not to say that abolishing the seniority system is the full answer. Because no matter how our dwindling resources are allocated, in terms of both ability and numbers priests on their own won't be able to manage the Church at local level.

In a preface to a new book published in 2003 - *Anglicanism: the answer to modernity*, Ronan Williams, the Archbishop of Canterbury, calls on his church to abandon its preoccupation with organisation and bureaucracy and begin instead to engage with 'a needy and confused society'. He suggests that his church needs to break with a managerial style of leadership and dismiss the obsession with administration or what he calls 'house-keeping'. Just imagine what the Catholic Church would be like if bishops weren't chained to their desks. Just imagine if, instead of priding themselves on efficient administration, they were to engage with 'a needy and confused society'.

Just imagine what a different ecclesiastical landscape it would be if promotion in the Church was on the basis of talent. Suppose too that we were able to leave aside all the bureaucratic paraphernalia, all the clogging officialese, all the empty titles, all the massaging of personal egos, all the peripheral logistics that consume so much time and energy and resources; just suppose that we were able to pare the Church down to one absolute priority – spreading the Good News.

Bishops in tandem with their priests, religious and laity would be encouraged to open a new page, to compose a short statement about what the Church is for and then to write out a list of those who can do what the Church seeks to do. Age, ecclesiastical honours, friendship with those in authority, a cultivated blandness, the qualities of Neil Kevin's *Safe Man* and the other unredeeming political features that facilitate promotion would be brushed aside. Talent, energy, imagination, creativity would suddenly find a new niche in the ecclesiastical sun. Those who were prepared to do the work would be given the opportunity to do it. Those who weren't or couldn't would be given duties appropriate to their enthusiasm or retired gracefully.

Only a team ministry can supply the comprehensive range of qualities and abilities that people now expect from priests - holiness, liturgical nuance, competency in preaching, an involvement in organisations, administrative nous, computer literacy, skill in management, expertise in group dynamics, communicativeness, approachability, an ability to listen, to care for the old and to be sociable with the young.

CHAPTER TWELVE

The way we worship

The reformed liturgical books could not give the rites a living face and flesh, colour and style. Only particular assemblies can do that. Posture, actions, dance, voice, singing, poetry, music, clothes, images, buildings are the flesh and the face of the liturgy, which can only be embodied in a group in a particular place, time and culture.

Joseph Gelineau

THE priest blessed himself at the beginning of Mass and intoned, 'Today, my dear people, is the Fifth Sunday of Lent.' 'No it isn't,' a little girl in the front seat said out loud, 'it's Mother's Day.' That incident sums up the gist of what I'll be trying to say in this chapter: the awkward truth that our worship is failing to connect with people's concerns, failing to engage their attention. That disconnection between life and liturgy is reflected in negative comments about sermons, in the boredom teenagers experience in church (if they are there), in the popularity of that definitively Irish phenomenon, 'a fast Mass'.

Part of the difficulty is that people are so overwhelmed with stimulation, communication has become so professional, the boredom threshold has so lowered through the rapidly changing images on our television screens, that the drama of worship in church pales beside its secular counterpart. Often the result is that we have allowed our modern obsession with variety and difference to force on us an effort to entertain people in church rather than to connect with something deeper. So the presider, instead of leading people in prayer, can find himself trying to jolly people up or, for the sake of variety, introduce elements to obviate the dullness of the proceedings and the result is not a liturgy that engages people's interest but what Cardinal Hume once referred to as 'a loss of the numinous'. Silence, stillness, a reflective ambiance, a prayerful spirit are all effective parts of the vocabulary of worship provided that the person is engaged. The primary focus in liturgy is on connecting with people at a serious level.

That begins with understanding today's society and today's congregations. Whereas once the mood was accepting, subservient and uncritical, now the mood is quite the opposite. People expect and demand professional expertise in every other area of life and when they come to church it's inevitable that they bring that expectation with them. Clichéd sermons, sloppy presentation, bad reading, crackling PA systems, poor heat, even ineffective presiding, all lead to negative comment. As well as that the sense of loyalty to one's own place, parish and church is quickly disappearing as people search out an acceptable liturgy or live in a community where they have no real connection and sometimes no desire for any connection with their neighbours. The community dimension that sustained allegiances, including religious allegiances, is in decline. Add to that the growing sense of impermanence in people's lives, the modern struggle with sustaining commitments, the individualism that is becoming more typical of modern Irish life and the almost insatiable need for variety today. No wonder the weekend liturgy is bending under the weight of such expectation and demand. No wonder the central impulse of our weekend liturgies is not so much engaging with our people as trying to appease their minimal needs. No wonder so many lay people no longer attend because they are convinced that their Sunday liturgy has nothing to offer them. No wonder too so many clergy have unofficially given up on liturgy – even though they continue to go through the motions – because they have come to believe that the kind of liturgy needed is simply beyond them.

There are other concerns too. Fr Keith Pecklers, interviewed in *The Tablet*, suggested that, 'you can tell in ten seconds when the priest comes out at the beginning of Mass [if] he is presiding out of a spirit of deep prayer.' The most important thing about liturgy, Archbishop Rembert Weakland of Milwaukee wrote somewhere, is that it is symbolically the bearer of the transcendent. That frightening thought sets in perspective both the enormous responsibility and the enormous challenge that attends liturgy. It isn't just about good PA or an appropriate level of heat or getting through it within acceptable parameters. For those who believe, liturgy is a matter of spiritual life or death. So the liturgy we weave has to be a rich tapestry of many shades and colours and textures if it is to connect the divine and the human, if it is to bear the transcendent. A challenge that demands significantly more than a priest drawing continuously from his own well.

Ideally, in the liturgy, a creative fusion takes place that connects the mysteries we celebrate with the ordinariness of the lives we lead. Through the liturgy God speaks and reassures and heals and where liturgy happens, we sense that we are connecting with God. This seems a far cry from the minimalist tradition of Irish liturgy in practice, often little more than a profusion of words where the translated Latin Mass is read through with an eye on mere validity and orthodoxy. The more complex weave of liturgy as a language of faith – drawing on place, sound, silence, imagination, space, memory, movement, symbol, metaphor – is seldom attempted. The thin texture of a new rubricism, in effect, often makes do for the richer weave of a true liturgy.

Another difficulty is that those involved in liturgy pay too much attention to the heavy hand of church control. It seems bizarre, for instance, that the Roman Curia, the papal civil service, should exercise so much control over liturgical translations, as if the local church is not in a position to be trusted to make appropriate judgements. (And if the English-speaking church has difficulty in this regard, imagine the problem the Japanese have. A senior curial official in Rome, Cardinal Stephen Fumio Hamao stated recently, 'No one knows Japanese here [in Rome] but before being used, a text in this language must be evaluated by the Roman Curia.') So much for the Catholic principle of subsidiarity and the Vatican II theory of increased autonomy for local churches.

The effort to connect worship to the lives we lead has to take precedence over the minefield of Church rules and regulations vis-a-vis liturgy. The question, *What can we do?* is often asked at parish level in the sense of *What are we permitted to do?* as distinct from *What is it possible to do?* Priests generally, having left aside the tortuous rubricism of the pre-Vatican II liturgy, are still prisoners of the kind of rubricism that closes doors rather than opens up possibilities. It is not that the wisdom of the universal Church or the advice of professional liturgists should be lightly left aside but that the question shouldn't be *What does the Ordo say?* or *What would the Liturgy Institute in Maynooth recommend?* but *What do we in this parish need to do?* The measure of an appropriate weave of liturgy is not whether it keeps the rules but whether it effectively connects with life and whether it engages people.

At the beginning of this chapter I mentioned the discrepancy between the world of the parish priest who was directly plugged into the Fifth Sunday of Lent and the little girl who was plugged into Mother's Day. The experts would immediately come down on the side of the priest but realists would know that a liturgy that didn't advert to the prevailing focus on Mother's Day simply wouldn't connect with the experience of vast numbers of people. The fact is that while Mother's Day may be dismissed as a commercial invention by the business world the truth is that it's one of the great feasts of the year. To ignore it is to ignore a compelling impulse of our people - to honour our living mothers and to remember our deceased mothers. Maybe what we need to do then is, like for St Patrick's Day, to arrest our focus on Lent and to shape a liturgy around Mother's Day: to introduce special readings, to use the offertory procession in tandem with a commentary to emphasise the different aspects of motherhood, to have a poetry reading after Communion as a reflection on mothers, to ask every mother in the church to stand during the bidding prayers, to list all the mothers in the parish who have died during the last year, to give every mother a rose as she leaves the church.

I know liturgists will hold their hands up in professional horror at the very notion of interfering with Lent, of the sacralising of a secular feast, of the mish-mash (as they see it) detailed above. But the question is: who has the pulse of the day, the PP or the little girl in the front seat? And what focus will liturgy need to have to engage the congregation on that day? And hasn't the Church always taken over secular festivals and transformed them into key events in the Christian calendar? Where did Christmas, Lent come from?

In his recent book *The End of Irish Catholicism?*, D. Vincent Twomey writes about how secular France celebrates the Feast of the Assumption as a public holiday and suggests that we might make more of our feast-days as public events. This is more wishful thinking than serious strategy as anyone familiar with parish life and with the decline of the popularity of feasts like The Immaculate Conception or The Assumption would quickly attest. It seems a more productive and sensible strategy to sacralise the secular (as has been the long tradition of Catholicism) rather than to expect secular celebration of sacred events. Though all options need to be examined we have to keep living in the real world.

What we need is a focus on a number of significant liturgies that, spread over the year and presented at the main weekend Mass, take the pressure off the other weekend liturgies. What I have in mind are liturgies that connect with people's direct experience rather than meet people at an oblique angle. Like a springtime celebration of new life and new growth; a special liturgy supporting those involved in examinations; Mother's Day and Father's Day; in late November for the dead of the year; a harvest Mass of Thanksgiving; a Mass of healing, incorporating an Anointing of the Sick. And what we need are liturgists who will facilitate such liturgies by compiling a range of resources: suitable readings, music, parts of the Mass, bidding prayers, a sample homily, appropriate reflective pieces as well as a series of possibilities for engaging people's interests.

I know such a request will not be universally welcomed because liturgists seem to descend through a very narrow genetic avenue where concerns like the seasons of the year and a series of incomprehensible and effete liturgical values seem to limit their ability to bend with the constraints of the ordinary parish scene. But there comes a point when liturgists need to become less liturgically correct and more clued into what can be achieved at parish level as distinct from what's deigned to be necessary by liturgical experts operating at a safe distance from the real world.

For example, I have nothing against Saints Cyril and Methodius. They are, I believe, patron saints of Europe. Apparently Cyril started the translation of the Bible into Slavonic and his brother Methodius completed it. The latter died in 885 A.D., 'worn out by his apostolic labours and by the opposition of those who failed to understand his methods' (Ordo)!

Well, my problem with Cyril and Methodius is that their feast-day is February 14th. Yes, *that* day. And, with no disrespect to Cyril and Methodius, when I say Mass on *that* day, I feel that their memorial has somehow subverted what is now one of the great celebratory feasts of the year. St Valentine, a Christian martyr who died in Rome circa 270 A. D., may not have much going for him in the way of ecclesiastical clout but in the popularity stakes poor Cyril and Methodius don't get much of a look in.

There is a serious point here. Apart from Christmas and Easter there is probably no single occasion that generates as much interest, indeed passion, as St Valentine's Day. Yes, I know that again, like with Mother's Day, much of the hype is the result of commercial interests trying to optimise profits on greeting cards and the often gaudy and tacky paraphernalia that attend the day.

But the point is that here is a ready-made opportunity to link into an experience and a reality waiting for a creative liturgy that would speak to a generation focussed irredeemably on that increasingly imprecise word, love. Instead of having to drum up excitement, as we often have to do, to give some context to liturgy, all the preparatory spade-work is already done for us, weeks in advance. As the momentum gathers, all we have to do is not miss the tide. (In terms of drumming up a false excitement, I am reminded of the late Bishop John McCormack's famous enjoiner to his priests, in the run-up to the canonisation of St Oliver Plunkett and the parish 'celebrations' that were to attend that historic occasion, 'to do your best to horse up a bit of devotion to Blessed Oliver'.)

The liturgy would have to be unusual, different. 'Creative' is the elegant word but you know what I mean. Probably not a Mass. More a gathering with the emphasis on ambiance. Candles, scented if possible. Incense burning. Scripture, Readings from *Desiderata* country. Familiar love-reflections. Guitars. Love songs. Dance. Background music. A few cushions, maybe. Connecting with that mixture of excitement and vulnerability that is the St Valentine's Day experience. Not the O Antiphons, if you get my drift. And probably not for the faint-hearted. Or the liturgically correct.

There is a wider truth here. Good liturgy, like good politics, is always local. It has to be situated in the context of 'the real': what matters to people, what people invest energy and emotion in, what connects with a lived life. Otherwise it can be a form of meaningless posturing, an effete interest for the informed.

Liturgy sometimes presents as an esoteric pursuit, with strict rules and within definite boundaries. It can end up stifled and constrained by convention, tradition, predictability. Like an electric rabbit at a dog-track, it is functional and reliable in that it follows the same pattern. And I don't want to minimalise that. In her latest book, *Almost There*, Nuala O'Faoláin, who professes her disbelief in things religious, writes about the comfort she experienced from the repetition of the familiar at a time of deep, personal distress:

I was familiar to the point of indifference with Irish Catholic worship. It was a revelation to discover that the familiarity could mean so much to me now - that the slow rhythm of the unfolding of the Mass, The Confiteor, the Kyrie, the reading of the Gospel, could be such a consolation.

But, important and all as predictability, familiarity and repetition may be, they pale in comparison to the variety and life and sheer exuberance of the real thing.

So we need to become a little more daring liturgically. There are areas of life that are gasping for rituals and for a language to give them meaning and to help situate them in a faith-context. Should a Spring Mass in rural areas be an important feast? Should the Harvest Mass of Thanksgiving be the great event of Autumn? Should I say our Easter Mass of the Resurrection on Enniscrone Beach just as the sun comes up over Kilcummin? Is there a course somewhere that would help parish groups to focus on the emerging 'secular' feasts of our time and would provide some resources to meet a growing need for a less predictable, less formal, more 'feeling' liturgy? Would our liturgical experts be better employed devising and resourcing liturgies for special occasions - especially now that attendance at our weekend liturgies is declining significantly - rather than inhabiting an exotic and twee existence where they end up telling us what we are 'allowed' to do?

The example of ICEL makes the point. ICEL stands for the *International Committee for English in the Liturgy* and concerns itself with translating official liturgical texts into English. It is something of a standing joke in the Catholic Church for its inability to conclude its proceedings and the tortured nature of its deliberations. At present it is trying to finalise scripture texts for a new Lectionary and Missal and rather than loosening up texts to reflect modern English usage it is going back to original translations which will make reading and understanding the texts more difficult and which will upset those who believe that older forms of, for example, exclusive language are less acceptable. The presumption was that older forms of address in the liturgy - like *My dear brethren* and using the word *man* or *men* in scriptural texts when the more accurate and more acceptable translation should read *man and woman* or *men and women* - would be replaced by their modern equivalent. Apparently not so. We're back into how-many-angels-fit-on-the-top-of-a-pin country as the experts debate and as the church politicians wonder what's the most they can get past the appropriate Vatican congregation.

While many would accept that the present language of the Mass is simple, spare and unpoetic, reintroducing Latinate usage and rejecting inclusive language will produce not just disquiet but mayhem in parishes. Imagine the confusion and disruption if the present introduction to the Preface of the Mass

> *The Lord be with.*
> **And also with you.**
> *Lift up your hearts.*
> **We lift them up to the Lord.**
> *Let us give thanks to the Lord our God.*
> **It is right to give him thanks and praise.**

is replaced by (as suggested in ICEL's first draft)

> *The Lord be with you.*
> **And with your spirit.**
> *Let our hearts be lifted high.*
> **We hold them before the Lord.**
> *Let us give thanks to the Lord our God.*
> **It is right and just.**

The message seems to be that while ICEL fiddles around with the meaning of words and Rome insists on a fundamentalist response to modernity by aggressively enforcing the use of archaic and artificial terminology local liturgy groups will take more and more responsibility for determining and shaping their own liturgies. An example of this is a parish liturgy group, unhappy with the exclusive language of the preamble to the fourth eucharistic prayer, which suggested that a more appropriate and inclusive version might read as follows:

Father, we acknowledge your greatness:
all your actions know your wisdom and love.
You formed us in your own likeness
and set us over the whole world
to serve you, our creator
and to rule over all creatures.
Even when we disobeyed you and lost your
friendship you did not abandon us to the
power of death, but helped all to seek and
find you.
Again and again you offered us a covenant
and through the prophets taught us to hope
for salvation.

Allied to all of that is the growing realisation that the weave of liturgy has to pay more attention not just to the place *where* liturgy happens (in the sense of a warm and inviting ambiance) or to *how* liturgy happens (in a visual, creative and imaginative way) but to the concerns and compulsions of people, if we are to engage the whole person and connect with his or her world.

Professional liturgists, though not all of them, often seem to operate out of a belief that liturgy has to be shaped more in terms of the past than the present. It is as if they believe that the ebb and flow of modern life is too thin to carry the weight of the transcendent, as if Gregorian chant is superior to the music of Liam Lawton, as if incensing with the thurible is more appropriate than the weave of dance, as if the past is a more appropriate liturgical environment than the present. Liturgy is of *now*, not of *then*.

CHAPTER THIRTEEN

Spirituality

In religion, as in politics, there is a jargon to which my ears have been closed for many years. I found that I lacked the words for religious experience, and that the experience was more real than the language in which it is conventionally expressed.

Sean Dunne

I'M not sure if the Blessed Virgin Mary made it to Achill or not in the summer of 2002. She was certainly expected. In fact, according to reports, she let it be known for some time that she'd be arriving on July 25th, 2002. Knowing all that, we suspected that she'd have some harsh things to say about the way the world is going.

We're told that Our Lady only appeared once in Lourdes and once in Knock; it all happened a long time ago and no one knew anything about it beforehand. All very unsatisfactory but that was before computers and modern travel and big business. But now, it seems, to satisfy a different audience, she sends the word ahead of her, giving details of time and place and visionary.

It was the silly season, of course. So the media made the predictable meal of it. The day before it seemed every tabloid newspaper and every radio phone-in programme started setting the scene. Creating an air of expectation. Pondering the possibilities. Looking for someone to interview. Then, having created the fuss, they descended on the prescribed spot to get the freaky picture for the irreverent colour piece the following morning.

Not that this modern penchant for summoning Our Lady at will is confined to Mayo. I remember once being in a church on a dreary winter's day at which a visionary from overseas was attending. The place was packed but everyone knew that on the dot of 3.45 pm the visionary would leave the church and go to a private alcove where Our Lady would appear to her. Apparently no matter where she was in the world, Our Lady appeared to her at the same time every day.

The Blessed Sacrament was exposed in the church but when the visionary rose to her feet and walked to the alcove the eyes of the whole congregation followed her. After the apparition she returned to her seat. Wasn't it lovely, someone said to me afterwards, that Our Lord and Our Lady were together in the same church on the same day?

But while few, I suspect, believe that Our Lady actually appeared in Achill why did so many actually turn up? There are a number of reasons: an indiscriminate piety ('Sure it's not doing anyone any harm anyway'); desperation (the sick seeking release from sickness and pain); a childish spirituality (no one prepared to name the difficult truth); a lack of knowledge of our faith (no experience of adult religious education); curiosity (I'll be there just in case something unusual happens); a day out (day-trekkers moving on to the next interesting location); the scoffers, including the tabloid media and the media 'stringers' who see the whole thing as an opportunity to make a few bob; and, last but by no means least, a new kind of 'bad news Mariology' that has been shaped out of fearfulness and depression about the world.

The message is predictable, always the same dreary package. How could anyone imagine that the mother of Jesus would want to share such a depressing message? Unless we get our act together God will sort us out! What God? The God of the Old Testament smiting sinners? Hardly the Jesus of the scriptures.

My objection to this nonsense is not some kind of intellectual refinement or theological snobbery that contrives to dismiss popular devotions as somehow beneath a sophisticated and modern Christianity. No, this is about the damage done to a credible and theologically respectable devotion to Mary that is part of the Catholic tradition of faith and piety. This is making a mockery of one of the central figures of our faith whose status comes from her connection to Jesus Christ, our Lord and Saviour, and from her role in the history of our salvation.

This is about saying that devotion to Mary is an important and legitimate form of spirituality but it has to be set in the context of a theology of Church and an understanding of Mary's place in the history of salvation. Anything else is an abuse of a tradition of spirituality that is part of our Catholic culture and of our Catholic faith.

A more worrying feature of this new spirituality is that sometimes it can receive semi-official status in the Church. There is, for example, a tract in stark Marian blue called *To the Priests, Our Lady's Beloved Sons*, which some religious extremists of my acquaintance insist on pressing into my reluctant hands at regular intervals. The book, which runs to 800 plus pages and carries an imprimatur from an Irish bishop, is a compendium of messages purportedly received from Our

Lady. Even though the mother of Jesus is quoted verbatim and at great length, the messages we are told must be understood not as words spoken directly by Our Lady but received, under the form of interior locutions, by one Don Stefano Gobbi. A quick glance at the contents surfaces the predicable mix of a contemporary faith-crisis, the scandal of internal disunity in the Church and the apocalyptic nature of our time. That such a confluence has been part of the nature of things since the time of Christ seems to have escaped its editors. Every age, defining itself as it invariably does in terms of what presents as a previous 'golden age', is in crisis, and every church age is susceptible to apocalyptic exegesis. Such is life and such is the Church.

Quite apart from their uncertain status or their deleterious effects, semi-official dissertations, like that mentioned above, have spawned a symphony of similar tracts at local level. In my own part of the world a vision of Our Lady in a field in the dank, dark summer of 1985 (when the Blessed Virgin seemed to be visiting every second half-acre in every townland in Ireland) has produced a record of the experiences of visionaries and other associates. Over the hill, a self-styled house of prayer promotes the same agenda. A wretched pamphlet called *Read Me Or Rue It!* written in 1936 by an Irish Dominican is doing the rounds, causing consternation and not a little suffering to the vulnerable and the gullible with statements like

> *It was related to a holy nun in Famphluna, who succeeded in releasing many Carmelite nuns from Purgatory that most had spent terms from thirty to sixty years! Carmelite nuns in Purgatory for forty, fifty and sixty years! What will it be for those living midst the temptations of the world and with all their hundreds of weaknesses?*

In the foothills of church life, a variety of figures (official, semi-official and occasionally bizarre) pursue ministries and arrange liturgies which are at once popular, lucrative and, from most orthodox perspectives, beyond the parameters of acceptability.

The whole enterprise has a very pronounced theological deficit. Despite our penchant for trying to write straight with crooked lines, it is patently absurd that the more unorthodox manifestations can be justified on grounds of piety or good intention, particularly at a time when the intellectual credibility of church and by extension spirituality are so much at stake. Of course it is understandable that, at a time when the critical and the cynical seem to be given *carte blanche* by a hostile press, the endorsement of the pious is an encouraging if pallid recompense for hard-pressed authorities. Yet the question needs to be addressed as to whether at a time of entrenchment and re-evaluation, it is wise not to confront the latest examples of mariolatry and other cheap forms of piety.

There is a case to be made for encouraging a kind of reverent scepticism in matters spiritual. We need not just a filtering system to keep nonsense at bay but a way of living with doubt. Keats in a different context talked about what he called 'negative capability', the ability to live with uncertainty. And that's about it. The credulous and the zealous try to close off avenues of doubt and uncertainty, to reduce everything to a simple formula of words or a set prayer-form, to banish confusion and unease, to restore order and discipline and clarity, to argue away the sense of displacement, disconnectedness and dis-ease that are irreducible features of our time. So if the Blessed Virgin tells us what to do, it divests us of the inconvenience of personal choice and responsibility. If the tension in the Church is discomfiting, the antidote is to pray for the Pope's intentions. And a few apocalyptic visions will be enough to focus the minds of the wandering and the ambivalent. Nonetheless, it is a failed strategy.

In the present situation, sidelining intelligence is also a failed strategy. Teresa of Avila, when asked whether it was best to opt for a holy but unintelligent spiritual director or an intelligent but unholy one, responded immediately that all things considered it was the wiser counsel to favour the latter. A seminary rector of unfond memory used to say that he had nightmares about ordaining those he charitably characterised as 'holy fools' on the grounds that in later life holiness rather than intelligence was the more susceptible to wastage. The intellectual life, William McNamara writes, is 'the first step toward contemplation. As a mental discipline it empowers man to gather all worthwhile things into focus and to eliminate what is trivial, irrelevant or merely sentimental.' What Newman calls 'intellectual culture' has a special claim upon our 'consideration and our gratitude'.

This is not to idolise intelligence or condone the anti-devotionalism that followed the years of the Council. Rather the task is to differentiate between what Andrew Greeley calls the popular and high traditions, the first of experience and story, the latter the tradition of catechism and creed. And not just to differentiate but to allow the two traditions to critique each other:

> *the popular tradition will critique the high tradition for what often seems its bloodlines and arid rationality, and the high tradition will critique the popular tradition for its wildness, its unrestrained emotion, its transient and self-serving enthusiasms. Without the watchful guidance of the high tradition the popular tradition may slip over the boundaries which separate religion from magic; in the absence of the energy and*

*vitality of the popular tradition, the high
tradition will find itself talking to empty
churches.*

What has happened is that at a time when the stark
truths of the Council are being 're-interpreted' or simply
ignored to suit the present restoration, the popular
tradition is no longer critiqued. So an uncritical and
unrestrained enthusiasm lapses into a muddled
devotionalism, at the very least, and its political
equivalent, an unthinking fundamentalism. The failure to
draw from the well-springs of the Council a spirituality in
tune with the rhythms of our time, a spirituality that
responds to the hungers of the heart, has left us in our
present predicament. Organise a novena and the crowds
flock to it. Call the same liturgy any other name and
hardly anyone turns up. Spread the word that a healing
relic will be passed around and the church is full. Have a
healing service and the church is empty.

Unease with traditional devotions in the years after
Vatican II has given way to the anti-intellectualism of the
present age.

It is not so much that we have failed to adapt the
Christian message to this intellectual age but that we
have begun to accept that it is either unnecessary or
impossible. Yet our theology of Incarnation is that the
Word is made flesh at a given moment in history and that
the Word has to be subjected to analysis and
understanding in every age. It is not that we have to blend
chameleon-like with the colours of our day but that we do
well to interface what we believe with where we live. In
a Church drawing water from a drying well, we seem to
lack the appropriate resources to do this. One effect of
this is that the need for stringent analysis and intellectual
vigour in facing up to our present difficulties is often
trumped by the spiritual argument, the need for prayer. A
stark example of this is that in a diocese where the need

for analysis is obvious to everyone, where intellectual rigour is needed to address the most pressing logistical and other difficulties, the Ordinary insists that much of the time allotted to clerical conferences is spent in Eucharistic Adoration! It doesn't take much time to work out that what is given precedence is not the value of prayer but the seductive appeal of a spirituality that seeks to camouflage a pressing need. In traditional institutions, those in positions of authority invariably prefer the company of docile companions whose critical antennae are irredeemably blunted by a superficial spirituality. *Say your prayers, lads.*

The underlying problem is the effort to cope with change. While the Church has to be *semper reformanda* [always reforming itself] part of the difficulty is that reformers are almost invariably perceived as disloyal. The meek not only inherit the earth but are less ambiguously cherished. Our predicament is that while there's no doubting the present malaise and the need to connect with it, we are gradually becoming inured to the possibility of change by a spirituality which places the focus not on opening ourselves creatively to a range of possibilities but on personal failure and individual unworthiness. Tradition is seen as retrogressive, limited, stifling instead of selective, dynamic, creative. So rather than create an imaginative and productive link between life and faith, we retreat into a meditation on our own personal limitations, facilitating as it does a pious disconnectedness from the issues of the day. The old dualism between the spiritual and the temporal is taken out and dusted off again. The words of Henri Nouwen, written twenty-five years ago, have a prophetic ring to them:

> *I am afraid that in a few decades the Church will be accused of having failed in its most basic task: to offer creative ways to communicate with the source of human life.*

Coping with change means accepting the transitional nature of our time. The old ways are dying but we haven't succeeded in facing that reality much less in finding ways of replacing them. The sense of restlessness this engenders is characteristic of our age and it is exacerbated by our tendency in pressured situations to revert to the wisdom of the past.

An example of this is an obsession with the New Catechism. Even though it is no more than a compendium of Catholic doctrine and is itself a consequence of the Council, it receives an unwarranted emphasis in comparison to the Council itself. Another example is our failure to surface a spiritual fare that would resonate with the hungers of the heart and instead we revert to the Rosary, May Devotions and the First Saturdays. And what develops is an ever-widening gap between what people feel they need and what our religion is able to provide. As a result the hungry sheep look up, are not fed and gradually drift into the shadows.

So is it any wonder that our churches are emptying and that those who have their own voice - intellectuals, the young and progressively more and more women - are walking away from us? The perceptible decline in Mass attendance is no doubt due to factors like carelessness or laziness or our easy compromises with the world. But there is more to it than that. Whether the Rosary, the May Devotions and so forth were ever sufficient to satisfy the old, they are clearly insufficient to whet the spiritual hunger of the young and not so young who now find themselves drifting into other avenues. It isn't just that the young live in a world suspicious of the search for religious meaning but that the language used to facilitate that search lacks either energy or depth. What irks too is that we have as a church a tendency to flatten experience, to push it through an institutional sieve, not to appreciate the individual wayfaring of the human spirit and the unique shape it may take. Coming as we do from staid

and settled traditions, putting a premium as we do on
fitting everything into traditional categories, we lack the
confidence as a Church to trust difference, to meet
experience at an angle and to accept that we can't always
make it fit.

We could end up as a wallpaper church, a bland
background to blend into rather than facilitating a
rainbow of colours where there is a niche for everyone on
a broad canvas and where different viewpoints are held in
creative tension. Part of the difficulty is that, in the wake
of current and recent scandals, as a Church we have lost
our collective nerve.

In that kind of atmosphere, nostalgia for the glories of
the past becomes a kind of anthem and a reactionary and
fundamentalist spirit begins to make hay. So defensive
ramparts are built, the old body-soul dualism, like a great
security blanket, gets another airing and we retreat back
into our churches to say the Rosary, waiting for the
storms to abate. Analysis is unwelcome, the prophetic
voice is stilled and we begin to lead from the back.

So an easy consensus emerges around a prayer-life
that insists on retilling the arid ground of the past because
it doesn't know what else to do, around a language that
has no vocabulary for the compulsions of our time. Yet
the spiritual impulse is alive and well, searching for new
religious forms because the old forms have been found to
be redundant no matter what nostalgic gloss can be put
on them. We recognised this truth after the Council when
we tried to reshape our sanctuaries into spaces for
authentic liturgy, when we deepened our awareness of the
different levels of consciousness at which we operate,
when we began to understand a bit better the
interconnections between the social and the personal
dimensions of our faith, when we almost succeeded in
burying the dualisms that had blinkered and blighted our
understanding of so much for so long.

But now the restoration is here and a version of the

past is being sponsored for our attention. The hideous statues are coming back. Tabernacles, in another appalling act of liturgical delinquency, are being restored to exactly the wrong place behind the altars. We are being encouraged to re-engage the litany of dualisms that we had almost expunged from our consciousness. Our parishes are being flooded with the most dreadful and potentially poisonous 'spiritual' literature and all sorts of codology masquerades as prayer. It is a time for reverent disloyalty not submissive servility, for the long view not the convenient fix, for intelligence not simple-mindedness, for the rigours of critical analysis not the pretence that all is well, for the two edged sword of the Scriptures not the balm of tradition, for a pure change to happen. Some of us, who remember the excitement of the days after the Council, thought it had but the moneychangers got back in. But now we know - and yet the dream lingers.

CHAPTER FIFTEEN

Yesterday was always best

There are now several seminaries training young men to celebrate the Tridentine Mass exclusively - and their vocations crisis is that they don't have room for all the excellent candidates who come forward.

Nick Lowry

SOME years ago I was invited to preach at the annual Knock Novena. I was given the theme: a sense of sin. Some friends immediately advised me to make sure I tailored my remarks for my audience. Those who attend the Knock Novena in their thousands every year are, in the main, elderly and traditional in their faith. Don't upset people, was the general advice. To ensure that I didn't I gave my text to a friend whose judgement I trusted. His response was, 'Well, that's safe enough, anyway.' My main point was that Jesus died for our sins, that he loves us beyond all our imaginings and that our sins are forgiven through his death on the cross. I went on to say that once forgiven we shouldn't scrupulously re-examine our consciences or worry about sins we committed in the dim and distant past.

I guessed that in the congregation were many who struggled with an unwarranted obsession with their own sinfulness and an implicit belief that God could not possibly forgive them their sins. Anyone who works in a parish will know the tortured and phobic avenues that so many good people unnecessarily travel in terms of seeking forgiveness for their often imaginary sins. In an effort to lighten the burden they carried, I placed the focus pointedly and unashamedly on the love of God for each one of us.

Shortly after, I went on holidays. I returned a few weeks later to find that *The Irish Catholic* was sporting the jolly headline 'Fr Hoban and Hell'. Apparently a flood of letters had reached *The Irish Catholic* saying that I had said in Knock that there was no such thing as sin. As a result *The Irish Catholic* had published, without my permission, an abridged version of my sermon with an effigy of Satan superimposed on the script. Even though my original script bore little relation to the hostile and scathing letters published about me in *The Irish Catholic,* I was for a few weeks disparaging news. Even though I was offered a right of reply in *The Irish Catholic* - '*Would you like another visit to lion's den, Daniel?*' - I knew that the damage had been done.

For more than twenty years I've written a weekly column for *The Western People* newspaper. My readership is, I think the word is 'settled' and I try in my own way to hold up a mirror of change to the conventions and rituals of life in a very patterned existence.

I am not always thanked for my efforts. A coterie of the unchanging and the unchangeable upbraid me regularly for visiting all this change on them. As if somehow, great technological revolutions and vast cultural changes could be deflected by yours truly putting his finger in the great dam of life. The great swell of life's tide doesn't decide to ebb because we'd prefer it if it did, thank you very much, or because someone passes a resolution or issues a dictat. So I have collected over the years a distinctive anti-fan club who write me long letters in tiny hand-writing on foolscap pages telling me that unless I change my ways and sing from their tedious and predictable hymn-sheets, that I'll burn in Hell - and other jolly refinements on the same theme. So now no matter what I say or write I'm wrong. Hence the savage criticism in *The Irish Catholic*.

There is, at the heart of our Church today, a phalanx of right-wing, neo-conservatives who are unhappy with the Second Vatican Council and the twenty-first century and who see as their life's work efforts to turn back the tide in church and society. So anything that doesn't fit into their narrow view of religion and the world is attacked. They see conspiracies everywhere and they are particularly critical of priests like myself whom they regard as 'disloyal' and 'dangerous'. Mention words like sex or abortion or divorce and they lose the run of themselves altogether.

This is nothing new. Ten years ago, when concerns were first raised about the incidence of child sexual abuse in Irish society, the Department of Education introduced a programme for primary schools called *Stay Safe*. It was short, just six hours a year, but because it was about sex and education it became a prime target for the new right. Two main points were advanced against it: one, the incidence of child abuse was lower than some commentators had suggested and two, discriminating between abusive and non-abusive acts on the basis of feelings was too problematic.

In *Intercom* magazine Gerard Casey, at the time a

lecturer in UCD, rejected a statistic of one in ten and suggested a figure of .9%, or nine out of every 1,000 children. His conclusion was that therefore the *Stay Safe* approach was unwarranted. At the time I was a columnist in *Intercom* and I replied to his article. If the same figure, I suggested, applied to cases of meningitis, would setting at risk nine children out of 1,000 not justify some fairly dramatic intervention? I suggested too that while the true extent of child sexual abuse is impossible to establish, the prudent and responsible approach to an area so clouded in secrecy and denial, is to assume the incidence is probably significantly higher than the available statistics would suggest.

I also rejected Casey's second reservation that using feelings to discriminate between different acts would introduce confusion into the moral training of the young. I felt that this disjunctive, compartmentalised approach to life was not helpful, that feelings are important and they do help us to suss out values. And that the only protection a five year-old girl may have against sexual abuse is how she feels about behaviour that she can't possibly be expected to fathom. Blocking a programme that is designed to improve that protection was, I felt, a serious matter.

The *Stay Safe* programme, I concluded, was a sane, sensitive and sensible approach to a difficult and distressing problem and we needed to support that balanced middle ground against the knee-jerk reactions of those who wish to transplant us into the black and white world of the nineteenth century where morality could be worked out almost mathematically. Conspiracy theories, gurus from America and juggling with figures, I suggested, wouldn't achieve much except possibly to help block a programme that may offer some protection to abused children.

Casey's article and his reply to my criticism of it is a good example of the kind of knee-jerk reaction to almost any effort to introduce new sex education programmes into Irish schools or new legislation into the Dáil. There's no crisis in Ireland in the area of child sexual abuse even though the Irish College of General Practitioners, the INTO and the Department of Health had endorsed the programme and the psychiatrist Dr Art O'Connor had written in *The Irish Times* (16/7/93):

> *Hardly a day goes by now but we hear of court cases involving the sexual abuse of children by fathers, brothers, strangers, teachers and even members of the clergy.*

As if child abuse in Ireland was just a figment of someone's imagination, a conspiracy dreamt up by the mandarins in a government department to infiltrate the moral consciousness of tiny tots. Or that the *Stay Safe* programme would introduce child sexual abuse into Ireland the way television introduced sex. Subsequent events in Ireland, not least the clerical child sexual abuse scandals and the success of the *Stay Safe* programme in offering a measure of protection to children, cast Casey's reservations in a strange light.

I had no gripe with Gerard Casey because he argued his case but the same could not be said about some of his fellow travellers. And it was galling that over the years that many of those who argued against the *Stay Safe* programme, the subsequent *Relationships and Sexuality Education* programme, and took high profile positions in the various abortion and divorce referenda, were given such attention by the leaders of our church. It was only when the last referendum on abortion was lost through the misguided intervention of Youth Defence and Dana Scallon, the European MP, that many of the Irish bishops fully realised the mistakes that had been made. Church and country have paid a high price for not confronting those who may have meant well but whose narrow view is only part of a much wider picture.

Part of that picture is the anti-intellectualism of the Irish Church. There's nothing new about this. Brian Fallon, in *The Age of Innocence*, in which he assesses the state of the Catholic Church between the years 1930 and 1960, writes that during those years the leaders of the Church, 'didn't want a generation of independent-minded, highly educated literate laymen quoting Pascal and Mauriac, who might ask awkward questions and undermine the people's unquestioning belief in their priests.' The Catholic clergy themselves were, Fallon writes, 'often naive – an admiration for G.K. Chesterton, for instance, was equated with mental sophistication, and the bulk of them regarded modern thought as predominantly "pagan" (a favourite word of the period), dangerous, and subversive, part of the corrosive modernism which was eating away at the foundation of the whole Christian world.' And then when the Second Vatican Council arrived with its ferment of ideas and its injunction to engage with the world the Catholic Church in Ireland, after decades of conformity, mediocrity and moralising, was incapable of taking the tide. The restoration policy in church matters in recent years has exacerbated the endemic anti-intellectualism of the Irish Church.

What Matthew Arnold once classically described as 'getting to know, on the matters which most concern us, the best which has been thought and said' is, in our illiberal institutionally-driven times, a debilitating, rather than a freeing, factor. Ideas disturb, upset, disenchant. So the rise of an educated, theologically literate laity – despite a public relations spin to the contrary – is perceived as threat not benefit. And the difficulty of coming to terms with the subtleties and complexities of modern religious belief is conveniently side-stepped for the more superficial pieties of parochial Catholicism. The critical, self-deprecating perspective that is needed in today's world to satisfy minimal criteria of coherence, complexity and authenticity has fallen on hard times.

There is no strong, critical tradition in Irish Catholicism. There is no MacHale to challenge the episcopal middle ground, no 'one man to die' for the Church. Whatever critical voice sought to articulate the questions that lie beneath the surface of Irish Catholicism with that modern balancing of independence and self-doubt, irony and hope, has long been silenced. The theologians who surfaced issues beyond the obsessively black and white religious experience of bygone days have been pushed discomfitingly to the margins or found refuge in more congenial climes. The few bishops with the intelligence and perspicuity to understand the need for a more informed debate were sidelined. The result is an unexamined self-doubt festering at the heart of Irish Catholicism.

So where does that leave us? When we find modern resonances of Graham Greene's literary progress from ambiguous agnosticism to disillusioned humanism, do we live with the difficult questions or revert to the casuistic safety of a ghetto theology? When the young - who like Joyce's Stephen Daedalus, are saturated with the religion in which they profess to disbelieve - contrive to apostatise from the faith of their fathers, do we travel that impatient road with them or do we self-consciously revert to the security of a Catholic culture disintegrating before our eyes? When frank discussions are called for on matters at once personal and significant, do we demonstrate a willingness to enter deep waters or do we lapse into a vacuous *bonhomie*? When efforts are made to present reservations about papal encyclicals as a form of non-belief, have we enough of a sense of history to know that such unease or even disagreement does not compromise membership of the Church. When reservations are expressed about the birth-control debate, are we prepared to live with the dictum of Aquinas that answers which do no justice to the difficulties raised are not only useless but are also intellectually and morally dishonest?

It can be said, I think, that never before in the history of Irish Catholicism do we need the critical stimulus of intellectual debate more and never before do we find so many reserving opinion out of a decent respect for their own ignorance. For what do we priests, for example, read anymore? Certainly not *The Furrow* or *Doctrine and Life* - at least not in any great number. Possibly the occasional chapter (or paragraph) in the occasional book we buy or maybe the odd sound-bite from *Intercom*, though apparently anything more than a page tests our resolve. Poor fare indeed to nourish a faith seeking understanding in a confusing and complex world.

And there on the sidelines of the Catholic Church are the new right, those who see themselves as the Pope's battalions, insistently pushing the complexities of modern life though a narrow prism and doing untold damage to the Church and to religion.

Where did these refugees from the sixteenth century come from? How have they insinuated themselves into the heart of the Irish Church? Why do bishops give them so much time and attention? Why are they allowed to block every initiative of note that tries to shape a new church for a new century and for a very different Ireland? How have they such access to Vatican departments and why are their often silly interpretations taken so seriously? As Butch Cassidy said to the Sundance Kid, who are these guys?

CHAPTER SIXTEEN

The morning after optimism

Tradition doesn't have to weigh us down.
We weigh ourselves down with tradition,
With the past, with past failures,
Past forms, past perceptions.
We have made these things:
We can unmake them . . . .

New worlds wait to be created
by free minds that can dream unfettered,
Without fear, turning obstacles
Into milestones towards luminous glories . . . .

Ben Okri

A QUESTION that has engaged the minds of people inside and outside the Catholic Church in Ireland is: how could so many moral and intelligent men in the leadership of our Church have failed the victims of clerical child sexual abuse? Surely they should have recognised how wrong it was, how damaging it had to be, how deep-seated the condition was, how inadequate was their response. Yet, in truth, there are mitigating arguments: the very limited knowledge of paedophilia;

the lack of awareness of how deep-seated the condition is; the lack of understanding of the damage to victims; the denial involved; the instinctive reaction to defend the Church; the refusal to believe that colleagues could be guilty of such horrific crimes; the lack of any real input of lay people, especially parents, into the internal deliberations of the Church in relation to child abuse; and so on.

But a similar and not unrelated question today is: why have so many moral and intelligent men in senior positions in our Church known that so much was wrong and yet never said anything? They knew that the leadership of our Church was inadequate to the demands of the present time. They knew that the clerical club was actively refusing to allow the organic development of lay participation in decision-making processes. They knew that there were huge questions around celibacy and sexuality. They knew how isolated and at risk so many clergy were. Yet they said nothing.

One reason is that part of our clerical culture is to regard promotion as a reward rather than as a task, taking position as a compliment without accepting the responsibilities that go with it. This is why many senior priests in senior positions in dioceses around the country knew that something was awry and would even share that wisdom with their friends but felt compelled to reassure their bishop that everything was fine and that he himself was God's gift to the diocese. It was the done thing. Others colluded in that deception because there were parishes coming up and they didn't want to put themselves off-side. It would be unthinkable within the clerical culture, for instance, for anyone to stand up at a diocesan conference and name what to most priests would be a difficult but incontrovertible truth. Such an action would be dismissed not just by the authorities but by most of those present who knew it to be true.

What lay people sometimes don't understand is the

ethos of control that a bishop exerts over his priests. Or, more accurately, is thought by his priests to exert, because it has to be said that it is as much perception as reality. This accounts to some degree at least for the extraordinary lack of moral courage among priests. To some degree, because surely it's not the whole story. It is an indication of how controlled the clerical club is that men ordained for forty or fifty years who know the truth of a situation feel compelled not to own or name that truth. I named a few truths in articles I wrote over the years for *The Furrow*. I wasn't thanked for it of course, as I expected, but what was most frustrating was getting supportive letters from church-people in positions of high authority and of some influence who commended me for what I had written and encouraged me 'to keep up the good work'. If they had said what I had said, someone might have paid attention. If they had even written a short note in public support of my position it might have moved things forward. But their lack of moral courage or the pressure of the club didn't give them that freedom.

A number of Irish bishops in difficult positions - some of whom have inherited legal and moral mine-fields from their predecessors - are simply not up to the task. We all know that but no one will name it. We know too the damage it's doing to the church. We know how dispiriting it is to priests working in parishes. We know that lay people are wringing their hands in frustration as their leaders score own goal after own goal even if we're ten nil down and playing into the teeth of a stiff wind in the second half. And we know too what happens to those who are prepared to name unpalatable truths. Fr Seamus Ryan of Cashel diocese and one of the most respected priests in Ireland, was elected President of the National Conference of Priests of Ireland (NCPI) in the mid-Eighties. The NCPI had come into existence because a previous body called the Association of Irish Priests (AIP), representing a group of liberal priests in the 1960s, was issuing radical statements on a variety of issues. Cardinal William Conway famously remarked at the time that 'we left a gap', meaning that the bishops should have foreseen that priests would have wanted a voice so the thing to do was 'to fill the gap'. The antidote to the radicalism of the AIP was an association representative of all the clergy of Ireland. At a conference in 1986 it was agreed that representations be made to the Papal Nuncio at the time, the late Archbishop Gaetano Alibrandi. At the now historic meeting in the nunciature in the Navan Road, Alibrandi told Ryan that he [Ryan] was 'a nobody representing nobodies'. This insult to the priests of Ireland scarcely caused a ripple in the Irish Church. It was the way things were.

In January 1994, Fr Kevin Hegarty, a priest of Killala diocese and then editor of Intercom, an in-house priests' magazine controlled by the Irish bishops, published an article by a Limerick social worker, Philip Mortell, warning against impending problems with clerical child sexual abuse. Now looking back it seems an important, even prophetic, warning but at the time Hegarty lost his job over it. Prophets are alright in the Old Testament but their status in the Irish Church is regarded as somewhat problematic.

People like Ryan and Hegarty are members of 'the awkward squad', those determined to insist on asking the awkward questions, regardless of discomfort or the pain. In another age, if it was well in the past, we'd call them prophets and surely if we've learned anything at all in the last miserable decade it is that we ignore prophetic voices at our peril. We need voices who will not be denied their space in speaking the truth because, in their myriad shapes and inconveniences, they provide us with a necessary focus, without which we can so easily lose our way.

But we've never quite managed to incorporate that sense of a loyal opposition in the Catholic Church in

Ireland. We dismiss our prophets as eccentrics, radicals, unwell, awkward and those in authority hope sometimes that they will simply go away. (A priest in a neighbouring diocese asked another priest whether he had read something I had written in *The Furrow*. His response was 'Has that fella not gone yet?' i.e left the priesthood). And we expect that the clerical club will distance itself from them and push them to the margins. Which is why so many priests are reluctant to name the truth. It's not just that some couldn't cope with life if there wasn't the prospect of becoming a monsignor built into it somewhere. Or that, after a lifetime of bobbing their heads in approval at every official position or enthusiasm some are almost constitutionally incapable of using the minds God gave them. Rather it's a sense that a narrow understanding of 'loyalty' doesn't allow for any kind of dissent, even if it's only saying what they believe or know to be true. It's a cold place out there on the periphery.

Dissent in and for the Church has a long history. Theologians of the old manualist tradition of moral theology accepted the possibility of dissent from authoritative, non-infallible teaching of the Church's magisterium. Some even maintained that this 'possibility' could become an obligation. As Charles Curran once argued, 'for someone who perceives such cogent contrary reasons that to maintain assent would be a perversion of his rational faculties'. But we're not talking about dissenting from authoritative statements here. This is about recognising that a true loyalty to the gospel demands that as baptised members of our Church we have a right, a duty, to name the truth as we see it.

The Church is not an end in itself. It's function is to preach the gospel message of Jesus Christ. And it's the responsibility of every generation of baptised Christians to shape its structures so that it becomes the optimum agent of that message. Which is why I want to proclaim a fuller loyalty by setting out my stall for a very different

Catholic Church in Ireland:

- a Church that's a garden rather a museum, a garden where diversity is cherished and difference celebrated rather than a museum where tradition is static and the past is glorified;
- a Church which welcomes and celebrates change, recognises what is dying and tends the new shoots rising from the ashes;
- a Church that can tune into the rhythms of the age, recognise the forces of democratisation as the most potent in our culture and adapt and reform its structures to reflect that force;
- a Church that honours the teachings embedded in the documents of the Second Vatican Council and implements them in the spirit intended;
- a Church that is prepared to name the truth, regardless;
- a Church that recognises the darkness within priesthood and is prepared to explore and change the church rule that links priesthood to celibacy;
- a Church that recognises the centrality of priest and bishop but doesn't accept that all authority and decision-making has to be reserved for a clerical club or that that club has a veto over the growth of God's Church;
- a Church that accepts the need for new forms of authority and leadership;
- a Church where respect for women goes beyond mere words and accepts that the ordination of women is a debate to be opened up not closed down;
- a Church that honours the dignity of each faith-community by resourcing and freeing the way we worship from the constraints of the past;
- a Church that finds new forms of the sacrament of reconciliation, new ways of ministering to those in irregular marriage situations and explores new ways of praying;

- a Church that refuses to be brought down cul-de-sacs that lead back to the sixteenth century and that resists the restoration of old ways;
- a Church where all the baptised, including the clerical Church, will find their voices and honour the melody that comes from the symphony of voices that God intended his Church to be.